SUMMITS AND SECRETS

KURT DIEMBERGER

Summits and Secrets

translated by Hugh Merrick

HODDER AND STOUGHTON
LONDON SYDNEY AUCKLAND TORONTO

British Library Cataloguing in Publication Data

Diemberger, Kurt
   Summits and secrets.
   1. Diemberger, Kurt   2. Mountaineers – Austria –
   Biography
   I. Title
   796.5'22'0924   GV199.92.D/

   ISBN 0-340-32427-9

CONTENTS

ILLUSTRATIONS

between pages 160 and 161

MAPS AND SKETCHES

NOTE ON TERMINOLOGY

Frequent reference is made in this book to 'four-thousanders' and 'eight-thousanders'. These are terms generally used on the Continent to describe mountains of 4,000 metres or 8,000 metres and over, respectively the highest summits in Europe and the Himalaya.

Etriers (*Fr.* literally 'stirrups') are miniature rope or wire ladders used for overcoming overhangs; they are secured to the face with a *piton*, a metal spike driven into the rock or ice.

Abseiling is the technique of descending a face on a double rope; and a *Dülfer* seat is an early method of organizing the double rope when abseiling.

Prussik-slings are loops made in the climbing rope, in which the feet are placed to facilitate the ascent of a vertical pitch, thus forming a rudimentary *étrier*.

PART I

The Astronaut

When the first man in space caught sight of the earth, his first conclusion was that it really was round. He next observed that it was surrounded by a shimmering blue cloak, clearly defined against the darkness of the void. Not one of the many stars he could see, not the moon, nor the sun, flaming unnaturally there in the black sky, evinced this fairylike feature. Only the earth – man's heaven.

Day and night succeeded one another swiftly. The speed of the flight was breath-taking, but the astronaut was not conscious of it. In the death-like silence, the earth turned beneath him. Now the strip of atmosphere stretched orange-red about the star, veiled in the darkness of night. Scarcely an hour later, cloud-banks were glittering in sunlight. What had become of Time? It was with a sense of irony that the astronaut looked at the face of his watch – except for the capsule, his only fixed point . . . oceans and continents filed past down below. There were people down there whom he could not see, and those he loved were just as remote. All he knew was that they were thinking of him then – there, under the blue glass-dome.

Some day, somebody, perhaps his great grandson, would fly still farther afield, right through the stars, traversing infinite distances away from the earth. He would know no more of nights and days. With him there would only be the stars, space and the fear of death.

What would be that man's thoughts? Must he not be oppressed merely by the idea of his immeasurable distance from the earth? Would he not live, out there among the myriads of the stars, in the sole hope of a safe return to it? To his earth which, for an inexplicable reason that lay in its very self, had created a paradise in the vast loneliness of space?

Our astronaut looked down again at the ever-receding earth. He too belonged to it; to the narrow, precarious space between zero and 8,000 metres, where man can live – in which all the world's miracles and all its bestialities are enacted – the glittering skin of a drop of water.

Down there under the magic carpet of the clouds, men were fighting and making love; in the loud din of war, tanks were roaring through the sands of the desert; ships sailed the seas and cities grew to being; here a mother was bringing her child to life, there a professor was cracking his head over the meaning of existence; forests rustled, and a young girl discovered that her breasts had started to form; and somewhere, somebody, cursing the whole world, died soon after. The earth kept on turning, and there was no end to love . . . for human beings beneath the heavens . . . who have always longed to go to where earth and sky meet.

And so they set out for the horizon, and climbed the highest peaks. Only wise men and lovers stayed where they were; but no one else understood why they had no need to go so far afield. Not even our astronaut, who had not climbed up to heaven, but burst through it, so that he was now outside, and could see the earth in all its limitations – and space in all its infinity.

A turntable was racing round. There were children, holding hands, cutting capers, dancing in a ring, shouting, laughing, clapping, singing in unison with the loud-speaker: 'Little Marcello has gone up into space in his space-ship with a special mission, and is now happily breaking up the stars with his hammer.' A roll of drums, and the stars splinter in the mirror above the gaily-hued pasteboard-box. Manfredo, aged just two, has fetched a chair and is looking on, entranced. '*Ancora!*' howl the others, for the record has run out; the little 'disc-jockey' – yes, he knows how – plants the needle back at the beginning, and for the ninth time the bright-yellow cardboard ship mounts with Marcello to the sky. And the whirling dance goes on . . .

Out here in space all is silence; the earth down there turns soundlessly. The man in the space-capsule knows that the moment for the descent is near – down through the blue cloak of vapour, which protects the earth from death-dealing space. Meteors are quenched in it, so heavy is it; human beings can breathe and move in it, so light it is. The astronaut knows it: in a few minutes he will himself be hurtling through that sky like a meteor. Then the heat-shield will begin to melt, the capsule itself may start to glow . . . and he, will he be burnt to death?

Everything has been worked out to a hair; he will come down safely to earth.

But will he? Nobody knows. Downward tilts the capsule.

Who knows how many urgent prayers have risen to heaven while men were hurtling back through the atmosphere?

Prayers, yes – but to what heaven? Where is that heaven?

The astronaut has landed safely on earth.

Crystals

Suddenly, the first wave of the *föhn* burst upon the silence of the valley. We were on our way to look for crystals, in the night, and the storm howled around us, throwing wave upon shock-wave into the vale.

The wind came from the south, roaring over the sub-alpine ridges, swirling far up to the Marmolata's crest, coursing in wild gusts among the pillars of the Drei Zinnen, and finishing by whistling the whole gamut of the scale among the ridges and towers of the Dolomites.
It was as if the whole sky had burst into turmoil, that March night. Was the storm ushering in the spring; in the night, of all things?
The white wall of the Hohe Tauern, confronting the warm southerly gale on its northward path, drove it high up into the sky. But it was not as easy as that to stop the 'Snowgobbler', as these storms are called in the Salzburg dialect. True, its cloak of cloud, caught between the ice-peaks tarried among the summits – but the storm itself fell with undiminished fury upon the valleys to the north.
There, in the Salzach lowlands, the night-dark meadows stood starred with the first flowers; spring was already here.
Suddenly, the first wave of the *föhn* burst upon the silence of the valley.

We were on our way to look for crystals, and the storm was howling around us. Why had we come here by night?
One of the locals was responsible for that, telling us that he found crystals much more easily by night than by day: they blinked at him from far off in the light of his lantern, as he climbed the gullies in the steep slopes . . .
The *föhn* threw wave upon shock-wave into the vale. They came roaring down from somewhere high up among the glaciers, tearing through the forest, and hastening away from towards the Salzach.
We could see very little, here in the pitch-darkness of the lower Sulzbachtal, which rose, narrowly confined at this point by steep slopes, towards the Gross Venediger – that silvery three-thousander rising

above the broad glacier realm of the westerly Hohe Tauern. Even when a gap appeared in the black wall of the forest, we could only guess where the peak stood, high above the head of the valley.

What an idiotic idea, searching for crystals by night ... I should never have thought of it, even in the days when, as a lad, I ranged the valleys with my hammer, dreaming of hidden rifts crammed with crystals. On the other hand if the local was right, it would be like a fairy-story. We had thought of that – already imagining the crystals winking at us in the light of the lantern – when we decided to pursue this fairy-tale.

So here we were, following the narrow path, which I remembered from my young days as a stone-hunter. There was a place where we had to turn up through the forest to the foot of a cliff. It was at a bend in the path, soon after crossing a brook. Could I find it in this darkness?

'How much farther?'

'I'm not sure. Maybe half an hour, maybe an hour. One moves more slowly by night.'

'Can you remember the place?'

'Yes, I shall find it again.'

Things had changed a good deal. Clearings had disappeared, the forest seemed to have grown denser, or was it just the darkness? The path, definitely the only one in the Untersulzbachtal, had not changed at all. Over there, in the next valley, there is a road now; and in the Felbertal – two or three parallel valleys to the east – today you can drive straight through a tunnel, on a splendid motor-way, down to the Dolomites. I am sorry about the Obersulzbachtal – I used to go there on foot . . . it was there that, twenty years ago, after a two days' search, I found my first mountain crystal. There it lay on the moss, clear as a drop of dew – just as if everyone knew that crystals always lie on a mossy boulder on a slope. I endowed it with an inner light of its own. Though there was no sun, it was brighter than the snows on the peaks. I can remember how my hand trembled as, at last, I picked it up.

My thoughts were interrupted . . .

'Do you think we still need the lamp? The forest isn't so dark here, and you say you know the way. We'll need it when we get there, because we can't find crystals without its light.'

'Quite right,' I agreed. I had a reserve flash-lamp in my rucksack, but it would be a pity if one of us couldn't see anything, up on the slope. So I turned the lamp off.

That moment, with the crystal lying there on the moss, still shines undimmed, whenever I recall it; even though I later found larger and more beautiful ones on the Sonnblick. Not even a shining green emerald

18

in the bed of a stream below an old mine in the Habachtal could oust that small, regular pyramid of quartz from its place in my heart. For it was my first stone.

Today, as I write this, I believe it to be quite wrong simply to believe that the new merely replaces the old. Sometime or other, in some place or other, the past will suddenly surge up – a person, a face, a likeness . . . a tune. And when it does, it is there. All of a sudden you relive something you thought long past. Sometimes it is only a recollection . . . but sometimes that past begins its own strange existence and grows stronger than the present. And so it becomes a new present.

Consciously or unconsciously? Who can tell, for instance, when a 'successful' man starts slaving away at taking a degree; when a dyed-in-the-wool bachelor marries the girl of his childhood, and a barrister decides to become a mountain guide? And then, it is by no means certain whether they themselves know why.

Even I remember an agonized rope-mate, whose ill-fortune it was that crystals suddenly appeared on a ridge we were climbing, and at more than one spot, too. I need hardly say that we did not climb our peak, that day.

'I believe I shall find a great big crystal today . . .' Yes, there was something in the air of this night, but what? I didn't know myself, so I laughed a little and said: 'All crystal-hunters believe that – I thought so myself, every single day. A hunter once told me about a wonderful great crystal in a rock-fissure in the forest; he used to go back every now and then to look at it. Only he knows where, though . . .'

'I can quite understand his keeping it secret. And why shouldn't today be just such a lucky one for us – on my very first search?'

'I hope it will be. It can always happen. But just now it's dark and we have still to find the place. The largest stones found on this face till now were about the length of one's finger – green, brown and sometimes even black ones, of quite unusual brilliance, possibly semi-precious. They are called epidotes, and, so far as I know, no larger ones have been found anywhere; and who knows what else may be hidden in the Tauern, unknown to anyone, even to the old crystal-hunters who clambered about up there for decades . . .' (not like me, for only a few days).

'Once – over there in the Habachtal – I had incredible luck myself. The two-man crew of the old emerald-mine had been washing for emeralds for days outside the half-silted-up hole in the face, at about 8,000 feet. They had already amassed quite a find of "collector's stones" – white or pale green crystals, all full of faults and flaws – but were quite contented. Pure, valuable emeralds are, of course, very rare and hardly ever found. The two men were very amiable, and allowed me to disappear, armed with a little luck and a big bucket, into the darkness of the tunnel. I could fill my bucket once, in the hope that, the muddy deposit might hold a collector's stone, in which case it would be mine to keep. I chose a place that looked likely and filled the bucket, at a venture. Once outside we separated the silvery mud under the jet of water in the sunlight. There, shone a collector's stone . . . and another . . . evidently my luck was in . . . And then, suddenly, we were all three staring in amazement at the mesh: on it lay a glorious emerald, dark green and full of fire, with not a flaw in it . . . Nobody spoke; but I knew what was coming next – I should have to surrender the stone. My luck had lasted just that short moment.'

The whole forest seemed to be in motion by now. The dark trunks swayed slowly back and forth, while the branches moved restlessly up and down, as if they did not belong to them.

'I wouldn't have given it back,' said the voice by my side. I did not reply. Odd characters, these trees all around us.

'How did you, a climber, take to searching for crystals?'

I hesitated. 'That's rather a long story,' I said, 'and had nothing to do with climbing, originally. But if you really want to know . . .?'

'I do.'

'Well, it started like this. When I was a child, my father took me along one day on to the Kumitzberg near Villach – a little, wooded hill at the gates of my home-town in Carinthia. There were supposed to be red garnets up there – whatever they might be; but I realized from the way he spoke that they must be something very special. We got there, after a long time; they weren't anything very special – just red blobs in the rock. What impressed me most was that I had had to walk so far; and my father was very disappointed with me.

'Later, however, at Salzburg, other stones began to mean a great deal to me; there was a big river just outside our windows and its broad rubble-covered flats, which changed in appearance completely after every high-water, seemed to us, when we came out of school, much more important and exciting than all the lovely town, with its parks, churches and fine architecture. On the "Salzach-rubble" nobody read us any lectures; it was our island fastness in the middle of an over-regimented life. No peaceful citizen had ever summoned up the energy to climb down there and interrupt our stony and watery warfare.

'One day I found a fossilized snail as large as a bread-plate in a lump of red rock down there. That gave me a new idea; each flood-water of the Salzach brought something new down with it and, gradually, more and more of it was transferred to our house. At first my mother was none too enthusiastic, but she was a woman who loved the sun and the woods and, indeed all nature; and, after I had shown her the snail, she left me to my own devices. I was soon battling for space; for the Salzach brought quite a lot down on its long journey from the Hohe Tauern to Salzburg. My father, just back from the front, sat in a prisoner-of-war camp, and I could not see him. But I could write to him; so, while I was alternately rustling up food from the Americans and hammering away down on the rubble, I kept him posted about my latest finds. He commented back on them and one day, to my great surprise, he sent me a sketch-map. It seems he knew where the red snails were to be found! I went there the very next day, going on foot with my map, as I did not then possess a bicycle: it was only three miles to the south of Salzburg. At the bottom of a deep red ravine I found quantities of what I was looking for – a whole sea-bed of snails, ammonites, crinoid-stems lay there between the ferns and the roots. Every time I found a new creature, the population of that sea-bed grew in my imagination. Even in the town I went around with staring eyes, and many of those who met me thought I was in a trance. How could they guess that, for me, a nautilus or an ichthyosaurus had just swum across the Residenzplatz? In spite of the heavy traffic, I felt absolutely justified, and certainly no dreamer; it had really happened – only, a couple of million years before. Indeed, someone had once found an ichthyosaurus in my ravine; but that had been a long time ago.

'Every Sunday I scrambled around on the steep cliffs of the gorge; very unsafe ground, slippery with clay, tufted with grass, and at some places dotted with scrubby trees. Twice I lost my hold, but managed each time to grab a branch before going all the way down. As I never met anyone between the walls of the ravine, I soon came to regard it as my own private realm.

'I was wrong, however. I had just gouged an ammonite, the size of my head, out of a newly-discovered ledge – it was narrow and I had to keep my balance by hanging on to a root – just climbed down and stowed it in my rucksack; was just ready, in fact, to whistle my cheerful way home down through the woods, when – as if sprung from the ground, a weatherbeaten old boy popped up, not five paces in front of me, regarding me with a knowing kind of look. Unable to find words I just stood and stared at him, as if he were a ghost; but he was very much alive. "Found owt today, eh?" came the amiable enquiry, emerging from that creased and crinkled face.

'"Oh, just a thing or two—" I stammered, diving into my trouser-pocket for a couple of crinoid stems.

'So there was someone else! The horrid thought crossed my mind that he might know about my ammonite-place up there. I followed an

21

ancient mushroom-hunter's precept: better say nothing. I show him the stems. I could feel the weight of my rucksack tugging at my back.

'"Not much luck, then, today!" said the old man, with an amused smile. "But tha's reet well equipped – so well" (and here he began to chuckle) 'that tha' dids'tna git oop to th' ammonite-layer oop theer – 'cos of t'load tha's wearin' on tha' back . . ."

'"Oh, I see," said I, greatly relieved; and then we both started to laugh. We collectors had reached an understanding.

'Two days later, I was visiting the old man, to see his collection; and with the undeclared intention of picking his brains to the best of my ability. He lived in a somewhat rickety house at the other end of town. Every corner of the room I entered glittered and sparkled, as if the dwarfs of the Grimm Brothers had brought their whole treasure up from the bowels of the earth. There were blue, red, green minerals; stones of every kind, size and shape, and more remarkable, something not to be found anywhere round Salzburg – marvellous crystals, of every shade and colour. At first the old man was just friendly, but said little: only that the crystals came from the Hohe Tauern. Gradually, I dragged more and more out of him; he told me about the old Roman gold-workings near the Bockhardsee, the emeralds in the Habachtal, all about crystals, dark and light, and also about our own epidotes, here in the Untersulzbachtal. He had suddenly become communicative, and told me a great deal about his expeditions to the rim of the glaciers, about ridges which no one visits. Yes, he said, there must be unimaginable treasures still hidden in the Hohe Tauern. As he spoke, my imagination was increasingly seized by the idea of the giant crystal hidden in some rift and waiting for me to find it. At the end of my visit, when the old man presented me with a coloured map of the Venediger Group, I was for starting out that very instant . . .'

'Did you ever find your crystal?'

'No, but only because I did not believe in it long enough. Had I done so, I would simply have gone on till I came across it. But I was lured away by the mountains, the Himalaya, Greenland . . . all the same, it might get a grip on me again any day; if so, I shall just grab my hammer, and go after it.'

For a while, the only sound was that of our footsteps. Then I went on: 'Do you know, there is nothing, however big or mad, you cannot achieve, if you believe in it. You can climb an 8,000-metre peak, cross the Atlantic alone in a boat . . .'

'If your lungs are up to it, and you have a boat, of course.'

'In the end, you can do anything. The only difficult thing is to get across to people. They have to understand you. Their hearts and souls are no mountains, no oceans; they are islands, waiting and hoping for the moment to come. Sometimes, they do understand you . . .

'Of course, not everyone can climb Everest – why should they? They may have discovered quite a different secret: a formula, a work of art – even, perhaps, in so doing – themselves.

'I wonder how many Hillarys and Tensings have never found their way to the heights, simply because they did not believe in them sufficiently? Maybe some descendant of the Vikings, on his Sunday afternoon walk, looks longingly at the waters of some river that winds down to the sea, and knows he is due in the office next morning. That is where he belongs in the "programme" – by his own volition . . . Or *did* he will it? Resigned, he goes home, to watch television, on whose screen he finds what he has lost; the wide, wide sea and far-off, unknown shores. And he waits for something – but what? Finally, he shakes his head, this son of the Vikings, has a look at the papers, and goes to bed. After all, there is always one's leave to look forward to . . .'

'Do you climb mountains, then, just because there is no "programme"?'

'Maybe; but I can't give any precise reason. It is simply that I am happy there, and so have to go back again and again. Sometimes the main attraction is that of the unknown.'

'When did you start?'

'When I was sixteen; soon after I met the old crystal-hunter.'

'And why?'

'I don't really know, now. It just happened, on a day when I wanted to hunt for crystals – in fact I was on my way to a source the old man had suggested to me . . .'

'And then what happened?'

'Nothing – except that I left it unvisited and went straight on to the summit.'

'Do you know why?'

'No.'

The forest had fallen silent. Over on the other side, or down in the valley bed, there was the rushing echo of a torrent.

'If you can't tell me why you went on to your summit, can you describe what it is like to be on a glacier?'

'I love it. For me it is the direct antithesis of a street. It is continually on the move; and you can wander anywhere you like about its ice; for only the glacier itself, with its crevasses and séracs, constrains you. But with enough experience and a good rope-mate, you can climb the most savage ice-falls . . . and how exciting it is to move among these fantastic structures of green ice, over outsize bridges, past towers the height of a house, through a fan-like tracery of blue crevasses, that changes from day to day! There are times when you hear a muffled crack in the giant's cold body; it has moved a little, again; or the roar of collapsing séracs. And when you are jumping a crevasse, you can hear the water down in its depths . . .'

'And you haven't fallen into one yet?'

'No – not yet, surprisingly enough, but, of course, one is always roped. So far, at the moment when I felt the ground give under me, I have always been able to crook my knee and throw myself across. Though I did once fall into a water-hole, quite early on, when I was a boy – and I was alone at the time. I had climbed up on to the ice, out of sheer curiosity, to see what it was like up there, and found it quite fantastic. I wandered about between the glacier-streams and huge mushrooms of rock and ice, occasionally throwing a glance over to the boulders on the moraine, in case there might be a crystal lying among them. It was early morning, and the sun had only just arrived; so the water-holes in the glacier were still hard-frozen. They looked like rare flowers – for the long blue-green stems of ice-crystals had, during the night, grown inwards from the rim to the centre, star-fashion. The sun mounted in the sky, and for once I suppose I was careless: I stepped on to one of those blue flowers, and found myself standing up to my neck in water. For half an hour afterwards – a shivering Adam – I hopped around and did exercises. Fortunately, there was the sun's warmth.'

'And did you note that "blue flowers" can provide a nice cold ruffle for your throat?' came from my side, in gentle irony.

'Naturally,' I answered, unable to suppress a little smile. 'But is that any reason for my not going where they grow?'

How and why did I climb my first peak? I find it difficult to explain it today.

It was the first time that this lad in the Obersulzbachtal, scrambling around at the edge of the ice and on its moraines, saw the great white summits rising opposite him – those great white, shining peaks. He had never seen anything like it before.

Here he was, hunting for crystals, but stopping again and again to look upwards, into the blinding brightness of the peaks. There they lay under a dark sky, so near and so utterly at rest. The snow up there belonged to a different world.

Suddenly, a dull roar filled the air and, from high up on the ridge, a stream of white poured down on to the glacier bed, shaking it far and wide. No, for this lad, there could be nothing more remote than those white summits. They were different from anything in his experience. He looked at them, deeply conscious of their inaccessibility; yet, at the same

time, recognizing their beauty of shape – the regular ridges of the Gross
Geiger, forming a pyramid – then the iridescent glitter of the Gross
Venediger's icefalls, the gentle sweep of its summit, far withdrawn . . .

It was all so unearthly and so vast that he could not understand how
anyone could go up there; on that dazzling white world there seemed to
lie an absolute taboo. And yet people did go up there. The peaks looked
down on him and held their peace.

Disturbed, the lad's thoughts went winging to the highest finding-
place of which the old man had spoken; a saddle in a ridge, nearly
10,000 feet up, in between two summits. On it there were phrenitic-
crystals to be found – a glittering pale-green lawn of star-points – and
he would very much like to have some. Should he really go up there?

The saddle stood high above the Habachtal's glacier-basin and there
was a rib running up to quite near it. One evening, he decided to go up.
He packed hammer, chisel and some food into his rucksack, and set out
at sunrise. The hut-keeper had lent him a pair of snow-goggles.

The white flank below the ridge was scored by avalanche-tracks; the
masses of snow had come to rest in the hollow at its foot. Slowly the boy
went up towards it. The rib was not very prominent, but looked safe; it
consisted more of rock than snow. Right at its start, there lay a lump of
crystal, big as a man's head, streaked by little dark-green chlorite blades.
What a pity it was broken . . . did it come, he wondered, from the vein
of quartz up above? But when he got there, there were only scattered
spots. He climbed on, over boulders and pitches; till, presently, the
sound of the waterfalls at the glacier's tongue grew fainter. And the
silence built up around him.

He put on his goggles, for everything was now dazzling-bright. The
snow-diamonds glittered. He had never been up so high before. To the
left, above him rose a summit . . . lovely, up there in the morning sun,
and in some way secretive, though the boy could not say why. He went
on up towards the saddle, which drew nearer. So did the summit.

The air about him sparkled. At every step he felt himself penetrating
a realm unlike any he had ever visited; everything seemed marvellous –
the view, the depths below, the very air itself. Far below, now, lay the
glaciers, the valley, the forests through which he had come, the broad
scree-cones, where he had searched for crystals. On the snow-slope down
there, he could make out a tiny trail - his own trail.

Yes, he had discovered something, but was not yet sure what. Was it,
perhaps, that he could move about up here – move most marvellously?
He thought of climbers. Was this it; was he meant to go on up – up into
that inaccessible world of summits?

That world of summits . . . one of them stood there above him; had stood all morning, with its brownish-grey individual structure of bare, shattered rock, rising out of dazzling snow-fields. 'A 'three-thousander', this; and, seemingly, quite near . . .

As the boy stood there, he could hear water from the melting snow hiccoughing among the boulders. Otherwise there was no sound. Up there, the brown rocks, the highest rocks of the summit, were powdered with the sheen of freshly-fallen snow.

There was something very odd about those rocks . . .

Yes.

Suppose he went on up there?

Yes.

And the phrenites? He looked across at the saddle in confusion. Tomorrow, perhaps—?

Yes.

But me? Me, to go up on to a summit? Me? thought the boy, in amazement.

Yes.

And now he wanted it; now he meant to go. Yes, I meant to, and have meant to ever since.

It was wonderful. I was the only being for miles around, and now I was going up the ridge to my summit. It had not changed an iota; but I had. Suddenly I was full of restless excitement about the unknown quantity of those blocks of rock up there. Rock which could, after all, only be rock – rock, above the snow and beneath the sky. I climbed on up the ridge for more than an hour – the summit was not so near as it had seemed – my joy increasing as I saw the intervening distance diminish.

The initial rib had long ago disappeared into the depths and I was working my way up between airy towers, of the strangest stratification; many of them looked as if they would fall down any minute. Far down on the other side I could now see a blue tarn and, much farther down, the Hollerbachtal. There were many peaks all around me, and clouds – everything had opened out into vast distances . . .

A step in the ridge pushed me out on to the slope, where there was wet, slushy snow. I traversed cautiously, digging now my hammer and now my chisel into the surface at every step. Suddenly, a little corner of snow broke away under me, grew into a slab of ever-expanding dimensions, broke up and carried away more snow with it. The peace that had reigned was violently replaced by a swelling roar. That is all I saw of it . . but from far down below I heard a wild turmoil and uproar . . . the roar of an avalanche. I stood rooted to the spot, unable to grasp it all.

How glad I was when I felt good sound rock under my fingers again.

And the summit had drawn appreciably closer. Suddenly, I came upon a green vein in the brown and grey of the rocks of the ridge – a mass of slender, shining needles, all in confusion, or in little delicate clumps like paint-brushes. I wondered what they were, and broke off a lump or two to take along, then continued my climb.

Then came the slab – the slab on which my nailed boots suddenly slipped – and I found myself, I don't know how, sitting a few feet farther down, on the edge of a cliff above the slope. And then I noticed that blood was gushing out of a cut in my wrist – slowly, in spurts, quite a lot of it. There followed long minutes of terrible fear. I lay down and held my hand up high – that might help . . . It stopped.

I lay there for another quarter of an hour, then I wound a handkerchief round my hand and felt my way forward with the other. I was close to the summit now, and sure that I would get there – a wonderful, overpowering certainty. Nothing could stop me now. A few minutes more and I should be there.

There were rocks, lying piled on each other, against the blue. Silent as heaven itself. Heavenly still . . .

My excitement was indescribable, transcending everything. I could feel my heart beating. Only those rocks above me, and then . . .

They were only rocks, after all. But I was up, up on the very top! High above an infinity of air . . . up on my own summit.

Nobody who has ever stood on the 9,885-foot Larmkogel in the Hohe Tauern can have any idea what it meant to me. For it is an insignificant mountain. But it was for me my first summit, and at that moment it belonged entirely to me.

In the south-west a fairy-like gleam broke through the brown of the cloud-wrack: that must be the Gross Venediger. The sun beat down. The silence was absolute, almost oppressive. Only the melting snow gurgled and guggled. How huge the world must be! Those were some of my thoughts at that moment – they have not changed since. Was that the beginning of it all?

To the north, the blue walls of the Limestone Ranges rose above grey-green, slabby hills of the Pinzgau. I recognized the Hochkönig by the light streak of its summit snow-field. Then there was the Steinerne Meer. At my feet lay the Habach and Hollerbach valleys, and far away to the east bulked a snowy peak, with a sharp, slanting summit – the Gross Glockner?

Clouds kept on hiding the view, clouds that came from the south, sweeping through the sky at about 10,000 feet and getting caught up among the loftier summits. I waited a long time for the Venediger to clear, but in vain.

At times a cloud would approach the Larmkogel itself, and then I sat for a while completely wrapped in white mist, till the wind chased it from the peak and it sailed away again, like a ship, over the deep valleys to the north, farther and farther, till it found some other peak to rest on.

'... peaks, unknown to me,' I entered in my diary.

The stars were sparkling and shimmering. There was the scent of soil and snow. We crossed a little stream, but not the one that led to the crystals. Slowly a fish-shaped cloud swam across the starlit sky, and the darkness deepened.

Just for something to say, I remarked: 'You're not saying much today.'

'No, but I see a great deal; have you noticed the cloud?'

'Yes,' I said.

It lay right overhead now, high over the tree-tops, like a baldaquin, vaguely defined and yet regular in shape, an odd cloud. Beyond it, the stars were coming out again. There was no sign of my cliff that housed the crystals. We went on. Wherever could that stream have got to? Perhaps it had ceased to exist?

More and more snow-patches between the trees ... We came out into a clearing, giving us an open view up the valley ahead. We saw the dark rocks of a gorge, pale streaks of snow, peaks rising above, hardly distinguishable. Definitely, no!

'What's up? Anyone gone wrong?' came a worried voice through the darkness, as I stood irresolute.

'Yes, we've come too far. Perhaps the stream has vanished – I don't understand it,' I had to admit. Ahead of us, in silence, lay the valley ...

'And yet you thought you still knew the way —'

Yes, I had thought so. I did not answer. What should I do now?

'Come, let's turn back, and we'll find it. That cliff is above one of those last ravines.'

We *had* to find it. *I* had to find it. Anything else was unthinkable.

Where was that face above the thick forest covering the slope? We went on up a gully: in vain. And yet it couldn't help being hereabouts ... or was it only a piece of self-deception, some crazy belief? So far, nothing but darkness and tall tree-trunks. Yet something kept on telling me it must be just here. We took to the next slope, a steep groove slashing up through the forest, filled with boulders, piled one on top of the other, often unstable and demanding care. Somewhere I could hear running water – feebly, faintly – a trickle, somewhere up above ...

The silhouette of a cliff loomed slowly out of the darkness, scattered tree-tops, dark against the sky, a cave . . . a slope . . .
We had found it.

All we needed now was luck.
As we were getting over the last boulders on the slope, we were delighted to find that our old local had been right: for suddenly, between the branches of a bush near by, there flashed a single splinter of crystal, caught in the hardly noticeable light of our lamp. This was the old man's conjuring-trick . . .
Anyone who has ever seen a ring sparkling suddenly in the darkness of a town in this sudden, unexpected way, must have asked himself how it could have happened. It could have been the light of some quite distant street-lamp that the jewel picked up and reflected.
And here, on a slope where every separate crystal lying on the surface reflects the light – how many surprises might lurk between soil and sand, stones, plants and the trunks of the trees? A slope-full of crystals . . . we shed our rucksacks.
Then, without losing another moment, we seized our torches and independently took to the slope. The *föhn* had diminished by now, and only came in occasional waves . . .
I was lucky. Flashes and sparks shone at me out of the darkness everywhere, and I hardly moved as I looked all around me. I have never seen anything quite like it. I only had to bend my head a little and in that instant there was the gleam of dozens of crystals, staring dumbly out of the darkness. I took a short stride, and enjoyed a new display of magic fireworks. It was impossible to think of searching. As I went slowly over the soft, springy ground, I was folded in by a void filled with secret sources of light – flashing, occulting, shimmering, increasing in intensity, vanishing, lighting up again – a sequence as fantastic as it was simple, as unearthly, and yet as of the earth, as is space full of the dust of stars, continually newly-born, flaming, dying out, being reborn – mute up there in the darkness. I was as thrilled as if I had found the crystal of crystals, though I was still empty-handed.
When I moved, this universe circled round me; when I stopped, the glittering orbit froze into immobility. Was I not, at the moment, a little God? And so I did not lay a finger on that magic world – it was beautiful as it was . . .
When, in the end, I approached one of these flashing lights and picked the crystal up, I found only a tiny splinter between my fingers!
I heard a voice saying: 'It's a little like your dreams.'
I couldn't help smiling. 'Yes,' I thought, 'but without them I would

never have climbed Dhaulagiri's shining glory, nor travelled to Greenland . . .'

I now started – with varying success – to approach individual points of light. What happens is this: the crystals glitter much more brightly through the dark from a distance than from near by in the light of the lamp. Moreover, it only needs one false movement, however slight, and the crystal disappears into the darkness, mostly for keeps. Nevertheless, there are no exact rules and since everything remains uncertain till the very last moment, what happens, again and again, is this:

You move, and suddenly, at a distance of about ten yards, there is a gleam among the leaves, growing swiftly in intensity – you stop dead, certain that this must be a big crystal. Very cautiously, and taking care not to deviate one inch from a straight course, you approach the alluring glint – for if you deviate, instead of a crystal, there will be nothing there but the darkness of the night. Just as you are getting near, a no less mysterious light shines out from somewhere else.

You remember that consistency is a virtue, and go straight ahead. When, at the end of it all, you hold in your hand a single flat object no thicker than your skin, all you can do is to think of a glow-worm robbed by an electric torch of its magic. Meanwhile, the other crystal has disappeared. Is one likely to remain consistent?

However, the chase of these glinting points of light was not always abortive. I finished with a handful of pretty little crystals. Some of them, poison-green, were like delicate needles, some black and step-shaped, others flat olive-brown prisms; all of them alike had a bright sheen. I remembered that people use these epidotes as jewellery, though not very often.

Shortly after – as the result of a further, highly exciting and successful hunt – I had a shining, empty, crystal-hunter's beer-bottle in my hand, my companion and I were sitting together at the foot of the slope, enjoying an apple or two, bread and bacon, washed down with a carton of milk. Between the silhouettes of the trees a pale glimmer shone down on us from the head of the valley, where rose the Venediger.

'Would you like to see what I found?'

'Yes,' I said, switching the torch on.

There were needles, flakes, prisms – more or less like mine. Not a single large crystal.

'Quite nice,' I conceded, turning a needle in the light of the torch. It shone olive-green and, immediately afterwards, dark-brown.

'Have you noticed how the colour changes?' I asked.

'No – how can it? Let me see!'

30

Crystals

'Watch,' I said, holding the needle in the blinding cone of light and turning it . . . green . . . brown . . . brown . . . green again.

'How is it possible?'

'It has some connection with the way the light falls on it and through it, and it only happens with very clear crystals – best of all with these small needles. This one will do it too,' I said, handing another one over. 'I have seen much the same thing with icebergs in Greenland; they change colour according to the direction from which the sunlight strikes them.'

The beam of the torch thrust like a finger into the darkness, lighting up a tree, or the ground, without rhyme or reason. Far up the valley we heard the echoing thunder of a springtime avalanche.

'Shall we have a go at the Venediger?'

'Do you think I could do it?'

'Yes, I think so.'

The light of the torch swept the floor almost horizontally. Suddenly there was a movement at my side, a couple of steps and a joyous cry: 'I've got it!'

I jumped up. 'What – a big crystal?'

'Yes, and so close to us. I suddenly caught sight of it, half-hidden under a stone . . .'

'Show me!'

It was a beauty. A dark prism, half the length of one's finger, with smooth, regular surfaces, simply laid against each other – but not symmetrical. A couple of fine lines ran along one edge, underlining its shape. It was a splendid specimen of an epidote.

'You can be unreservedly happy,' I said. 'There isn't a flaw in it.'

'I am,' came the answer.

The find had banished every trace of weariness. Wide awake, we charged up the slope again, as if luck and endurance have anything to do with each other. Or have they?

I have no idea for how many more hours we went up and down that slope. Perhaps it was only a single hour. If you ever ask a crystal-hunter how long he spent digging, or climbing up and down in his search, he will look at you with great surprise and give you a vague answer – for, among the boulders, minutes pass like hours and hours like minutes. One simply hasn't any idea . . .

It was still dark. I had gone back to the top of the slope and was pursuing my search there. I did not have much luck, but it gradually dawned on me that, on this day, it was of no such great importance. For during this night I had found more than ever before. It was as if the whole show-case full of crystals at home had suddenly sprung to life – in

31

a whirling, glittering orbit on that hillside, an orbit that was still continuing. It was part of me now – my great discovery. It was strong as the air blowing down from the mountains, from their summits; the air that blows from up there, where everything is so strong and inexplicable – as inexplicable as what was then being wafted to me on that air . . .

The boy I had once been – it was the same thing as made him go, that first time. A thing indescribable in words. A thing granted me afresh today, as if it had never been before. A thing that had always existed.

Yes, we had both found something – more than ever before. I remembered how I had ranged these valleys, in search of the great unknown. Perhaps a great crystal?

Was that why I had come here today? And you – why have I told you so much already? I hardly know you. Today you found your first crystal. That is almost all I know about you. Down there on the hillside, I can see the light of your torch shining. Why did I bring you here? Is it perhaps that in our very lack of knowledge of each other there lies an element of knowledge?

Down there, on the slope, the light of your torch moves back and forth; a circle of light in which a hand is sorting soil and stones, testing, rejecting, selecting . . .

Who are you? You, who enfold a thousand possibilities?

The light, its circle, moves and moves, erratically. At a movement of your head, your long hair suddenly falls across the light, a shimmering, shining curtain. Then the circle moves on again.

You remain the enigma.

Or have the crystals taught you some of the truth – about that boy? What would it mean to you if I led you up to some high summit tomorrow?

Will you ever be able to understand that the ridge, the icebergs in Greenland, and the Himalayan snows can mean just as much as these crystals? In that case, we shall not have come here in vain. But, perhaps you, down there on the slope, are only looking for a stone for a ring?

The wind had almost dropped; a chill air rose from the ground. I got up and walked up and down for a while.

'How much longer are you going on looking?' came up from below.

'I have stopped looking,' I answered.

'Then we could move on, couldn't we? I am tired and cold – and I shan't find anything more. Besides that one stone is so lovely – what more could I want?'

I slid down to her over the unstable slope in a couple of strides.

'You are right – let's go. But first show me the stone again . . .'

She undid her breast-pocket. 'Of course,' she said.

32

I could feel the nearness of her. The stone was marvellous. I began to think a little less categorically.

'A piece of jewellery,' I remarked; and the description fitted.

'Oh, do you think so?' She held it against her finger, her head tilted sideways, looking at it long and searchingly; and then still longer.

'It would suit you admirably,' I laughed, a little too loudly, and ran my fingers through her hair.

She did not reply. Then a little smile passed over her face. 'Oh no,' she said, looking at me, 'it's not like you think.' Then, suddenly serious and thoughtful, her eyes returning to the stone. 'It would be a shame. I will keep it as I found it – along with today.'

Dawn filtered between the tree-trunks as we came silently out into the Salzach meadows.

Behind us the night seemed far away and yet as real as the grass beneath our feet and the houses we were approaching. Early risers were stirring. The sky was like a turquoise.

We felt, at one and the same time, wide awake and very tired. Down on the road, the ground seemed to give under our feet at every step. I saw crystals – a firmament – full of brilliant flashes. And the day that was coming. The first rays of the sun touching the summit of the Venediger.

A happy certainty. Tomorrow we would be climbing it.

PART II

Grandfather's Bicycle

My grandfather gave me his bicycle, a 1909 'museum-piece'. 'Ride to school on it,' he said; and I can still see the stern but kindly face with its white moustache. He was a headmaster, and headmasters always have to be a little stern . . .

He had covered the whole of the hilly country around the little village in Lower Austria, where he had worked all his life, year in, year out, either on his bicycle or on foot; for he was a keen hunter.

When he was fifty, he thought he had perhaps done enough pedalling, and acquired a motor-cycle; but when the war ended, he had to dispose of it, and started pedalling again. He was still pedalling when he was eighty; and, had not the sight of one eye deteriorated, he would no doubt be pedalling today, when he is over ninety and still facing the world with great confidence.

That bicycle certainly opened up undreamed-of possibilities for me. What matter that this 1909 show-piece was one of the first to be made after the famous 'penny-farthings'? Or that it was still rather taller than normal machines, and a little peculiar to ride? That was just its hall-mark; and there were definitely three people who knew how to ride it – my grandfather, my father and I. Everyone else – and I had a number of friends who wanted to try it out – dismounted in great haste.

'Either you can or you can't,' thought I, and launched out on great adventures. My bike and I crossed the highest passes in the Alps together, journeyed far and wide through Austria, Switzerland and Italy.

I have it no longer. One day I left it outside the railway station, un-padlocked, as always. When I at last remembered it, two days later, it had disappeared, and it has never been seen again. Even now, I just can't understand it. Certainly, nobody can possibly be riding it. Perhaps it graces the private collection of some connoisseur as a vintage exhibit; or maybe, one of these days, I shall recognize a part of it in an exhibition of Pop-art sculpture.

Nowadays I belong to the majority of the human race – those who either possess, want to possess or have possessed a car. Nowadays, I too take to the available motorway and think in terms of mileage, petrol, cash, and time. A spin in the car? Yes, of course – why not, on a Sunday afternoon?

Yet I wonder whether mountains, valleys and passes really exist any more for the motorist? If anyone says they do, I hand him a bicycle and tell him to get cracking. I am sure he will very soon turn back – and will have understood the message. Poor devils! – he will be thinking – meaning the cyclists. Never again will he attempt a pass on a bicycle; but that will only be because he has sat in a car for too long a time.

Rrrums-treng . . . foot up, look up to see if the hairpin is clear . . . it is . . foot down . . *trrreng* . . then the next hairpin . . *rums-treng* . . . through it . . . left, *treng* . . . right, *treng* . . . left, right, left, right, left . . . ah, here we are at the top of the pass. The motorist is king of the world. He has done it again . . .!

Let's hop out for a couple of minutes and stretch our legs a bit, and look at the view. Noticeably colder up here, but the view is fine, really remarkably fine, the view; a cigarette, eh? Or a quick one at the bar? Yes, the car did very well; the engine still pulls splendidly, well enough, that is – but, of course, such a lot depends on the driver . . .

Then down again on the other side, *rums-treng*, the first hairpin, *rums-trrreng* the second . . . left, right, left, right, left . . . with a new sticker on the windscreen.

What's that I see – a cyclist? And – two more? Dear God, there must still be idealists about the place! The proud motorist at the helm maybe falls silent for a while – or he starts talking about the treadmill of our era, of the shortage of leisure time, of the treadmill from which there is no escape . . . the treadmill . . .

But perhaps, as I have suggested, he falls silent for a while and does some quiet thinking . . .

My grandfather's bicycle was a magnificent treadmill. When you trod on the pedal you took a giant's leap forwards, because the chainwheel was outsize. Later on I changed it for a smaller, more modern one. That produced an additional advantage: for I then had some spare links for my chain again, whereas I had been forced many a time to call in a blacksmith's skill on the old one.

At the outset, I rode to my fossil-beds – what an improvement that was! I was there in next to no time. How mechanical transport can alter one's life . . . a quarter of an hour's pedalling and I had covered ground which used to take me a long hour on foot, and reached my Glasen-bachklamm, the gorge with the ammonites. Farther north, it only took an hour to the sandstone cliffs of the Haunsberg, where long ago the sea used to break against the near-by coast, and where you could find sea-urchins as big as your head, mussels and a hundred other creatures. And, just before the end of my fossil-hunting days, fate granted me an unusual and highly impressive find. There, on a boulder below a sandstone cliff, in the middle of the woods, sat a crab, which chance had allowed, almost as if intentionally, to fall from high up in the cliff. I couldn't believe my eyes. There it sat, bolt upright, with half-closed claws, between the ferns and the shrubs, as if waiting for something . . . for 70 million years.

That sort of thing had, however, become a Sunday-afternoon pastime by now. As soon as I found a little more time, I rode farther afield into the Hohen Tauern, whose realm of peaks now lay open to me, without an upper limit; but I still kept on disappearing into its remotest corners, to look for crystals, minerals, or even gold – for the Romans had discovered the precious metal in the rocks of the Tauern and had mined it high up among them on the steep shores of the Bockart See. I found the gold-galleries, though they were barely recognizable. I must admit at once that I did not make my fortune, for what I lugged down to the valley was pyrites. Of course, I knew that, but I hoped there might be some gold in it. There wasn't. So, in the end, I dragged half a rucksack-ful – and all I could carry – of silver ore out of a gallery which, for a change, had been worked as recently as the Third Reich. I now felt that I had a great deal of silver at home. True, it had not been minted, but that did not seem to me to be important.

Then I climbed up again towards my summits, traversing the Geiselspitze in fog, armed only with a sketch I had made beforehand; for, having no camera, I had started making sketches of my summits. I had already sketched the Gross Venediger and the Gross Geiger, the first two really white peaks I had ever seen. I was also doing things quite near Salzburg. At Easter, I took a hammer and a chisel, and climbed the north face of the Schafberg, high above the Attersee. There were Christmas roses still blooming down in the woods, snow and ice above that, and finally rock. I felt dreadful, but I could not turn back, and got to the top in the dark. Today I would not dream of tackling it without crampons, and I shudder when I think of it – but young climbers in their early years have all the more need for an outsize guardian angel.

At that moment I discovered for myself a guiding spirit, though a wingless one: it was a book on my father's shelf. He had climbed a little himself in his younger days and later again during his military service. Over and again I had heard the story of his solo climb in army socks – he had left his forage-cap down below – on the Red Tower in the Lienz Dolomites; a story which grew more gripping every time it was repeated.

Sometimes, too, when some of his old friends came to see us, I also heard about a certain chimney, up which they had hauled girls from Lienz – by preference fat ones – and how entertainingly Mina had got jammed in it.

The book was called *The Dangers of the Alps* – and it was a fat book at that. There was nothing about Mina in it – but it provided information about absolutely everything else: cornices and avalanches, bad weather, belaying with or without an axe, chimneys and overhangs, snow-slopes and glaciers. 'The Dangers of the Alps' said the jacket, 'by Zsigmondy and Paulcke'. Clearly, at that moment, nothing more interesting could have fallen into my hands . . . It is a certainty that there could be no book of greater interest, and it happened, not infrequently, at school that the margin of some history-book suddenly acquired the picture of a rescue from a crevasse or a snow-contour or the stratification of some mountain – for it was clearly of decisive importance whether one climbed on the top of the strata or toiled painfully up the outward-sloping pitched-roof on the reverse side . . .

My history teacher did not approve at all; but what he naturally could not understand was that it is no use being angry with such people, for they cannot be other than they are. And so I got my usual gamma minus for history again. On the credit side, I owed my life to the three-point rule of climbing when, on an easy but exposed pitch, a foot-hold came away. And it still seemed to me much more interesting to know why a glacier breaks up into crevasses, why in its ice those extraordinary interleavings of blue lie between the paler strata, why and how cornices form, and how to cut a step. When my father presented me with an ice-axe and a rope, I was the happiest person alive. For now I had everything I needed.

And what about grandfather's bicycle?

It was still going splendidly. Why shouldn't it visit Austria's highest mountain-pass, the Glocknerstrasse, which climbs to over 8,000 feet, and where the sharp peak of the Grossglockner soars another 4,000 above the Pasterze glacier at its base?

The trouble was, I had no mountaineering pal, and I didn't dare go up so high by myself. All the same I set off with a school-mate who was at the time a keen cyclist.

We marched and pushed our way up the Mölltal. It rained pitilessly and Erwin and I envied the odd motorist. We were wet to the skin and we never stopped moving all day, so as not to catch cold. In semi-darkness, dead tired, we sought the shelter of an old rick. By morning the hay was wet, and we were dry. When we crept out of our marmot-burrows, we found ourselves in brilliant sunshine. True, it was cold and snow had fallen far down the adjacent slopes, but the road soon had us warm again, rising gradually and steadily as it did, finally in wide hair-pin turns. We dismounted and reverted to pushing.

Suddenly, at the far head of the valley, a white peak appeared. That must be the Glockner! But it was not long before another and higher one gaining in height as we drew nearer, lifted its head. We swore that one must be the Glockner, but we were wrong again. At last it really came into view, unmistakable in its sharp and slender shape, lifting high above everything else in a dazzling mantle of fresh snow. My heart rejoiced at the very sight of it. Then, mastering my excitement, I thought: 'Suppose I could somehow climb it!'

Next day I persuaded my companion (Erwin came from Hanover, in the plains) to embark on the ascent of a neighbouring 'three-thousander'. We made good progress up it and a tiny glimmer of hope for the Gross-glockner awoke in me. Meanwhile, this mountain of ours was appro-priately named the 'Sandkopf', which is exactly what it was: miles of debris-slopes and fine scree. Suddenly, I saw a crystal lying in the rubble and progress was abruptly halted. I dug down with both hands, working like a mole, and eventually found a couple more crystals. When I began to dig my fifth 'run', my friend started to show signs of discomfort. I assured him that it was my last but one, and he cheered up a little. After my fifth 'last but one', my finger-tips were wide open and Erwin, by my side, was complaining bitterly. It was late in the afternoon, so we turned back. Erwin was quite reconciled to his fate; far up in the rubble, he had found a horseshoe – heaven knows how it had got up there – and today he is a successful veterinary surgeon . . .

As we left the scree-slopes we saw something else for the first time ever: a whole meadow full of edelweiss, white many-starred clusters shining up at us everywhere, covering the whole meadow with a delicate veil of white. That evening I looked up at the Glockner with growing confi-dence: I didn't know how and with whom but somehow or other I should get there . . .

That inner feeling about 'yes' or 'no', which I used to have before decisive and often hopeless undertakings, giving me an answer in quite obscure situations, was to remain with me farther and farther into my life. Usually, the answer was 'yes'. Sometimes I did not trust it, and lived to regret my mistrust.

We were still ten miles from the Franz Josefshöhe, ten miles of mountain-road at a gradient of 12 per cent. When we got there, we would be 8,000 feet up and looking down on the grey-green ice-stream of the Pasterze. The Grossglockner would be opposite us, 12,461 feet high. It would take half a day's shoving our heavily-laden bikes, step by step, up those endless hairpins . . .

Next morning, when we left the little village of Heiligenblut, with its slender spire, we had become a threesome. A Viennese, by name Walter, had latched on to us. The important thing about him was that he belonged to the junior membership of the Alpenverein; so the summit of the Grossglockner had moved sensibly nearer. Proudly I showed Walter our edelweiss. 'Not bad,' he said, 'but they are cow-edelweiss – there are proper ones above the Pasterze.'

Cow-edelweiss, indeed . . . that same day we clung to the slabs and found the 'proper ones' – wonderful stars with slender white points. They lay like hoar-frost above their leaves, above the dull green of their stems, with their little yellow suns at the heart of each flower and the soft felt of their starry points, as clean and fresh as if they had just come from the laundry . . . then a clump of grass gave way . . . and I landed backwards on a ledge in the face.

'Stay where you are and don't move,' yelled Walter. I lay gasping for breath, my limbs numbed with fright. In the end, I pulled myself together and climbed up again; but I had had enough of edelweiss. Below where I landed, there was a drop of a hundred feet . . .

During the next two days, while Erwin went on a bicycle-tour over the Hochtor, the 8,200-foot summit of the pass, Walter and I actually climbed the Grossglockner. Even by its normal route it is a regal peak, steep, airy and exposed. No one is ever likely to forget the moment when he stands in the notch between the Klein and Grossglockner, with the Pallavicini Couloir plunging 3,000 feet from his toe-caps; and then, turning round, observes that there is a damnable amount of air below him on the southern face.

That was the first time I ever wore crampons, an ancient set of ten-pointers borrowed at the Franz Josefshöhe. 'Keep your legs wide apart!' Walter instructed me, as we worked our way up the steep slope from the Adlersruhe to the sharp-crested pyramid of the Kleinglockner, with the abyss deepening at every step beneath the soles of our boots. Suddenly – a crampon-point had got caught in the meshes of my stockings. There – oh, hell! – I stood balancing on one leg. Walter, belaying me undisturbed, laughed and said: 'What a thing! Now straighten yourself out and I think you'll have learned a lesson.' He was right, and yet it can happen to anyone at any moment, and there you are, poised on one leg like a stork. The only difference being that the stork is used to it, while you don't find it amusing. 'Keep calm', is the only answer.

My clothes provided a remarkable contrast to my ice-equipment – consisting as they did of a leather jacket and, of all things, leather shorts, to which I was particularly devoted. Later when, at the cross on the summit, cold mists crept around my knees, I insisted on our starting down again at once. Some hours later a swift descent on their seat had restored my faith in that article of apparel. All the same their days were numbered, and it was the Gross Venediger which finally tipped the scales . . .

Walter disappeared, as he had arrived, and I have never heard a word of him again; but it was he who made a present to me of my Glockner.

I was now seventeen, and my life had undergone a decisive change in a very short time. Ever since, four years earlier, I had found that strange fossil in my trench among the Salzach's rubble, I never let up in my attempts to master more and more of the world. The crystals had led me to the mountains and grandfather's bicycle had laid open for me the road to distant places. I knew I was only at its beginnings, but what joy it was to explore, to guess, to find out everything that might lie along it. The circle in which I knew I had been confined had no limits; it was up to me to extend it ever more widely, to reach out impatiently even beyond it in my imagination, always to be pressing forward to new objectives.

As I rode along the Salzach valley and looked into the lateral valleys opening up to the south, to where the green of the forests took on a bluish tinge, I saw white peaks in the distance. There were more than a dozen such valleys; at the end of each, a high mountain. The road to all of them now lay open to me. I went to one of them, the Gross Venediger, for reasons I need not explain. It was simply the high white peak up above the crystals. There I met some people on their way to the Grosse Geiger and joined up with them. It was an expedition on which I seemed to be breaking out beyond myself, so changed were things since 'a little while ago'.

The Venediger was not at all kind to us. Above 10,000 feet we ran into a blizzard. In spite of all the advice of the nice old keeper at the Kürsinger Hut, I was again wearing my leather shorts – my beloved old gear . . . I was already pretty obstinate, even then.

All the same, we went to the summit, where there was nothing but snow and storm; we had no view at all. My elation at getting to the top was soon chilled and killed by the gale which seared my bare knees. I clamoured for the descent. Very soon my legs were entirely covered by a garment of clinking ice-tassels. 'My poor calves,' I wrote later in my diary, 'lots of little icicles, one hanging from every hair. A proper pelt.'

I ran as much as was possible and, although they say that ice is an excellent insulator, I made a vow, on the spot, never again to go up high wearing the leathern rig of the chamois-hunter and the poacher.

A few days later, however, we saw the summit of 'our' Venediger as we had looked forward to seeing it. No, it was even better than we had imagined it would be; for that sun-drenched day was a very gift from Heaven, up there on the glittering snow, high above the valleys in their autumnal glory. One of those rare days you can hardly dare to hope for, ever again.

Willi, from Vienna, was the leader of our party. I had been deeply impressed, during the preceding days, with his ability to find the way even in the worst weather. He seemed to know exactly what was bound to happen in any given situation. He was pleased with me, the youngest member, who came up last on the rope, because I had twice stopped a fall, over there on the Geiger, by the speed with which I rammed home my ice-axe.

Between us went Eva and Trude, two girls from Berlin – and let me add at once that the mountains have nothing on Berlin girls!

Forgotten was the icy storm on the Venediger, forgotten my frozen knees, as if they had never been. We were all hot with excitement and expectation of the magic mountain rising before us. I remember winding my handkerchief around my axe, so cold was it as we moved across the glacier in the twilight of dawn. The Venediger loomed pale overhead, above the slender ribs of its north face and the curling cornices that swept up with its ridges. Under a velvet sky the snow drew a soft line across the broad saddle towards the Klein Venediger – yet another pyramid. The last stars were flickering. Each of us was alone with his thoughts, the rope our only link. And as we climbed slowly up towards the first icefall, my 'Voice' of those days recorded:

'Away to the east lay a tumultuous cloud-wrack, coloured from a marvellous orange to red and pale green. The sun was not up yet, the pale and misty sky changed from a steely grey to brilliant green and later to bright red and yellow. A dull sheen lay on the ice-armour of the Venediger's summit, lifting above the north face, deeply scored by dark runnels of ice. Where was the sun . . .? As though touched by some ghostly finger, the very tip of the Venediger began to gleam a delicate red; slowly the gentle light flowed farther and farther down the face, till the whole peak hung high above us, bathed in the brilliant morning light, while we were still in darkness. "The glacier looks as if someone had poured raspberry syrup over it," Trude remarked. The sun was up now; all the summits were now lit by it, only we were still in the shadow of the hollow. Would we too meet light and warmth up there on the saddle?

Here it was cracking cold, and my hand and the handkerchief froze to the steel of my axe.

'We were on the last slope leading to the saddle, going slowly up. The angle eased. Thirty yards ahead of me, Willi let out a yell of surprised delight: he was standing in sunshine. As I joined him, I almost had to close my eyes to meet the blinding flood of light that beset me and enveloped me, cancelling out gravity itself. Trude expressed that sensation when she said: "Now I'm floating away on the sunbeams." Our dark-blue shadows alone broke the shimmer and glitter of that virgin snow-slope; for we were the first to come up here since the storm. We were happy beyond description. The remaining peaks of the Venediger group rose out of the flood of light; far away soared the Glockner, and the blue world of spires over there, that must be the Dolomites. A world of savage turrets and walls, with the Drei Zinnen easily recognizable. The shadows, far below us in the valleys, could not even climb up to us; they simply disappeared under the flood of light. We felt weightless as we mounted the summit itself, halting there only briefly. Today there were no limits to the view: one could see right across to the Ötztal Alps.'

For us too there were no limits that day, not even for our cautious Willi. A wild euphoria had seized upon us all, as the four of us strolled, arm-in-arm, down the Venediger to the Rainerhorn, straight into the eye of the sun. The rope behind us dragged on the surface of the snow, but we didn't care. And we sang the song of the Tyrolese girl, which had become our Venediger theme-song: 'Hollariariaholadi – holadio . . .!' There in front of us rose the Rainerhorn. We bagged it, too, and celebrated on its summit with song.

Then across to the Hohen Zaun, the next summit. It was not till we were making our light-hearted way down on the other side to the Defregger Hut that we met people – a whole column of them, coming up, with slow and measured tread, as is right and proper. At least ten of them; a hearty crowd of women-climbers of the 'Touristenclub'. They looked askance and shook their heads at our casual procedures, but we were off and away by then.

That was by no means the end of our day – we dined on a few drops of glacier-water, some porridge-oats, lumps of sugar, and a swig of lemonade – then rubbed sunburn-cream on our lips again, for they were going altogether to pieces today. After lazing about for an hour high above the Defregger Saddle we crossed the Maurertörl and completed our circuit of the Venediger. By the time we reached the Kürsinger Hut, we had been out for fifteen hours. Our 'Hollariaria – holadi – ho – ladiho' in honour of the Gross Venediger sounded a little subdued. After that it began to snow heavily . . . In my excitement I had quite overlooked the fact that school had started three days ago.

If I have strayed somewhat from the theme of grandfather's bicycle, my excuse must be that so important a mountain as the Gross Venediger was responsible – and the blue world of the Dolomite towers rising above the glittering snow of the saddle . . .

My friend Peter and I had agreed to leave Salzburg and get to those Dolomites and, once there, to travel the length and breadth of that fairyland of rocky shapes. On our bicycles, of course. Peaks? Yes, some of those too – if possible. I could still see the stark faces of the Lienz Dolomites in my mind's eye.

We were just due to leave, when Peter arrived with death and disaster written all over his face. 'I can't come,' he said. '*She* says I have to choose between her and the mountains!' I was very sorry for him.

He lent me his Leica to take along and I promised to bring back some slides for himself. I had two colour-films – my first – to capture the meadows full of flowers at the foot of the Dolomites and the bright colouring of their rocky walls, as described to me by those who knew.

Milestones, milestones, milestones, rain, rain, rain . . . wet roads . . . rain . . . dense grey clouds, with dark lumps of limestone sticking into them . . . soaked through . . . all alone . . . and the Dolomites as wet as my climbing-slippers . . . push the thing uphill again . . . would I get to Cortina today? . . . anyway, what should I do when I got there? So far as I cared, the devil could scoff the lot.

I wondered whether I could latch on to a lorry, if one came past. Latch on, I did, and the driver didn't notice me. Well, now I should at least cover some ground; though what was the use in this filthy weather?

My goodness, he's stepping on it! Of course, it's level here, but it'll soon be going uphill again. Just you hang on! Crash, bang, splinter . . . I found myself hanging on the lorry's tail-board. It had stopped. My bicycle was somewhere underneath it.

The driver came round and helped me to get it out – I was almost in tears. The front wheel had had it in a big way, otherwise . . . no damage? Miraculous. What about the main members of the frame? No, only the front wheel. That was bad enough, though.

Two days later I left Cortina, with a bare 3,000 lire in my pocket, and pushed my repaired mount up towards the Falzarego Pass. It was drizzling steadily and the lumps of limestone thrust up into cloud, as usual. The whole of the Dolomites were soaking wet, and so was I.

At last a shape emerged from the veils of cloud – the Cinque Torri. I recognized them from the postcards. At least, and at last, I had seen a peak.

Some hours later, the clouds parted and the gigantic mass of the Tofana rose above them. What a mountain, what a precipice! And then, far to the west, there emerged a white dome. That must be the Marmolata, the only snow-peak in this realm of rock-towers.

At the summit of the pass I remounted, and flew down the wonderful road, with its finely built-out hairpins. Down and down I raced – it was quite fantastic. I was heading straight into the sun, now low in the west, under low banks of cloud. The road had flattened out. I met a few people on it, passed a few houses. A deep valley opened up on my left. There, to the south, rose an immense mountain – glowing ghostly red against the dark background of the sky: a dragon's spine, surmounted by spikes, looming longer and longer, a gigantic wall in the red sunset lave. Breath failed me, my brake squealed, as I drew in to the side of the road, bemused. There, to the south, stood that ghostly mountain, a mass of glowing organ-pipes, barring the whole breadth of the valley. An old peasant came trudging slowly by. 'What is that?' I asked him, and pointed to the great red wall. '*E la Civetta,*' he replied, as if this were an everyday occurrence, and continued on his way.

The Civetta. I never forgot her. Many years later, I was to return and climb that mighty face; but I will never see her again as I saw her at that moment.

Milestones, one after another, in the sunshine, as I pushed my bicycle up towards the Pordoi Pass, among the flowery meadows of the Dolomites, brightly lit by the sun, with the Tofana's summit now far away behind. There were very few cars; the sunny road belonged to me, as did the gigantic rectangular masses of the Sella group above it. So did the grasshopper which crossed the road in great leaps; and the snail sitting at the edge of the road near by, pointing its horns. For some unfathomable reason, it wanted to cross the road too. I picked it up and carried it across. Fancy having as much time as a snail! As a matter of fact I had. It was a gorgeous day.

Step by step, I went up on snow, with my ice-axe and in my rock-climbing slippers, towards the foot of the Boë-spitze, the highest elevation in the Sella group – a rock-peak, with a flat cone lifting above huge rectangular cliffs for its summit. I met more and more snow-fields, of hard frozen snow, with wet fresh snow lying on top of it. My leather shoes got wetter and wetter, and larger and larger – I had taken the 'old master' Paulcke too literally and left my heavy climbing-boots in Salzburg – larger and larger grew my shoes . . .

Finally, having got to the top, I dangled my feet, and my shoes too, in the sunshine. Opposite me, encircled by cloud, flanked by the sharp Vernel ridges, stood the Marmolata, with its broad white glacier, curving steep and massive valley-wards. It was quite irresistible . . . Below it the road twisted like a worm through the gaily-coloured Pordoi meadows.

But what could I do, without boots?

I stood on the Marmolata's summit, in climbing-boots as big as those famous Seven League ones. I had simply gone into a little inn down at the Joch and asked the innkeeper if he would lend me his boots for a climb of the Marmolata. Below me, the South Face plummeted in a fearsome drop to immeasurable depths. It must be awful to plunge to one's death from a Dolomite face . . . they were really no place for anyone but a good rock-climber, and even then they were horrific. Very carefully, hold by hold, I felt my way down from that airy view-point by the way I had come. In deep thought I went down the glacier and across the meadows, redolent with a cloud of cinnamon scent from the small dark-red flowers that covered them, to the Pordoijoch, where I returned his boots to the innkeeper.

The Karersee,* that small tarn, a perfect subject for a colour-slide. I took one for Peter, too. Crystal-clear turquoise water, its dark pine woods and the grey towers of the Latemar above.

I sat by its shore and gave my machine 'full service', surrounded by my pliers, my 'King Dick', ball-bearing-grease, oil-can, a cleaning rag, and a sparrow hopping around and complaining because I had nothing more to give him. This was a lovely place; I would push on in the evening – somewhere. Meanwhile, this spoke needed straightening, and there was the rattling mudguard-ring . . . Somewhere, but where? Perhaps past the Marmolata's southern base . . . look, here's another spoke . . . over the Pellegrino Pass to the Civetta . . . And then the carrier, always getting perilously bent: I should have to load it some other way, or find some additional support for it . . .

That Latemar, up there . . . its towers and turrets looking for all the world like recruits, the first time they are told to fall in and dress their ranks, with a certain natural disorder, a sort of irregular regularity, like the rows of pine-trunks rising from the other shore of the lake . . .

* In Italian: Lago di Carezza.

48

I won't move on tonight. I shall traverse the Latemar tomorrow. I want to see it from near by.

I did that, and a great many other things besides; and, wherever I went, everyone exhibited an interest in, and enthusiasm for, cycling which was quite new to me. They were very kind, and let me know that a cyclist was a highly-respected person in the Dolomites – even a cyclist riding his grandfather's bike. I was even asked for which great race I was in training; and I noted in my diary – 'Yesterday, as I sped full-tilt through a village, the children shouted at the top of their voices: *"Evviva Bartale! Evviva Coppi! Evviva!"'* I swung into the next curves with my chest proudly puffed-out, speeding, and feeling, like a champion, only slowing up again as soon as I was out of sight.

Of course, I sent a postcard to my grandfather: 'I have been promoted to the top class. The bicycle is still in one piece. Five Dolomite passes so far, and plan to do three more.' Certainly I had discovered and mastered the Dolomites on a bicycle; experienced, over and over again, the excitement of the unknown view that would unfold beyond the pass – a prize only to be won by long hours of hard work. But then everyone who loves adventure must be prepared to accept hard work – or he will lose both.

And many a motorist – perhaps I should add, many a mountaineer, too? – who thinks on different lines from the cyclist, must none the less realize that he who cheerfully surmounts hairpin after hairpin of a pass under his own steam, yet enjoys a great deal of pleasure in so doing, is totally involved with that 'mountain'; its summit is an aim which he has set himself, and when at last he gets there, great is his joy.

It goes without saying that riding down the other side, free as a bird and motorless, is sheer delight. But that is not all of it. The cyclist has his 'why and wherefor' just as has the mountaineer; though neither of them could explain it. And both earn their 'dimension' again and again.

The Matterhorn

AN EXPEDITION

The Matterhorn, that slender spire, lifting indescribably above the
Zermatt Valley – every climber's dream-wish . . . sketched, painted,
photographed, described in a hundred different accounts, familiar to all
. . . and yet only really known to those who have actually seen it . . .

Erich, Gundl and I had not seen it yet. For us it was a mysterious
mountain, clothed in legends, far, far away, somewhere over the
horizon, in an unknown land. To reach it meant, for us, a real expedition. We had never been to the Western Alps. We had no money; but
we had our dreams – dreams of unknown peaks, in unknown countries –
at least, those we could get to on our bicycles.

The Matterhorn . . . this legendary Matterhorn . . . this 'mountain of
mountains', over 13,000 feet high; no, nearly 15,000 – it kept on growing, this *Matterhorn*! Why not make straight for it? It drew us irresistibly;
though, of course, we didn't know how we should fare at such an altitude – we had never been on a 'four-thousander'.

By now I believed we could climb it. I had heard a lecture by the
'Dachstein Priest'. I did not know exactly who he was, but he didn't
look as tough as all that. If he had climbed it, we could!

It was a splendid lecture, entitled 'The Valaisian Peaks'. We were
introduced to the white wall of the Lyskamm, with its perilous cornices –
not that it looked dangerous, just white and beautiful – but if he said
so . . . Yes, after all, its crest did look dangerous, and it too was over
13,000 feet – yet another four-thousander, surpassing that magic level.

Why not combine the two targets – legendary Matterhorn and our
first four-thousander, both at the same time? In short, why not go
straight for the Matterhorn? If that cosy-looking old gentleman had
climbed it, we could. I marvelled at him; as he spoke, the mountain
drew ever nearer, acquired rocks, ridges, pitches, arêtes. Yes, we would
make a bee-line for this Matterhorn, making no détours, paying no
attention to other peaks, on the way . . .

The holidays came round. In front of me the big rollers of a colour machine were grinding away, crushing powder in clouds of green, blue and red dust. I fed the mixture, strictly in accordance with the recipe, and dreamed of the Matterhorn. I had taken this temporary job, so as to earn some much-needed money. The firm promptly went into liquidation.

So I went to Aunt Betty, who, I knew, had a kind heart. 100 schillings from her – well, that was a start. Then to Aunt Traudl ('Hallo, Kurty, glad to see you!'). Enough for the three-speed gear for my bike. Then to Uncle Hans . . . and . . . and . . . to all the relatives I could think of. With very few exceptions – and I suppose, in their cases, my failure to visit them before was responsible – they had all heard of the Matterhorn. Even if it wasn't Mount Everest, the expedition's funds grew satisfactorily. To all of them I promised a picture of the Matterhorn, for their living-room, their kitchen, the corridor – it was their problem where to hang it, not mine.

I believe Erich, who was eighteen, a year younger than I, was doing much the same; while our buxom Gundl, with the long plaits, who was only sixteen, was busy working on her mother, in their Styrian home, for the mere permission to come along. It was only when I drew up a detailed list of equipment and provender – 'the thousand minutiae' – that her mother realized on what a serious undertaking we were embarking.

We pedalled and pedalled and pedalled . . . we got off and pushed . . . we got on again and tore downhill . . . then we pedalled, pedalled and pedalled again . . . still not less than a week to our Matterhorn.

We entered this unknown Switzerland. Spit-and-polish houses, wonderful hotels, everything neat and tidy. Anyone who slept rough got himself fined. The passes were high, the peaks higher still. And the prices . . .! We post-war Austrians couldn't believe our eyes. That didn't bother us, however. We lived on our rucksacks, boiled our tea at the roadside; our 'bikes' were amply loaded with what we had brought along – everything we needed.

Push, push, push – all the way up the Furka Pass, which we reached on the stroke of midnight. Our impatience to see the Matterhorn knew no bounds – a shepherd over there on the Oberalp Pass had told us that one can pick out its summit from here in clear weather. Well, we should just have to wait till morning. Now, to find a site for our tent . . . This was a puzzle, for the heavy rubber-coated 'Special' tent my father had given me had no struts – presumably because its designer was an optimist. It had a loop at the top, so that you could hang it up somewhere . . .

We wandered about the dark summit of the Pass – we would gladly have hanged the designer of that loop from the sickle-moon overhead.

We found no hooks; so we lay down and crawled into that chilly skin. The only ray of light was Gundl, in between us, comfortable in the fleece sleeping-bag. My knees were gradually coated in hoar-frost, but my back, at least, was warm. During the early hours, Erich devised several suitable methods for liquidating our clever designer.

Up came the sun . . . we stood there with chattering teeth, looking at the dark rocky summit in the dim distance, hardly distinguishable between whi e ridges. There it was, at last, the Matterhorn . . . still miles away.

'A cup of hot coffee?' This was unbelievable. A friendly man in field-grey uniform had come out of a house at the roadside and invited us in. However, when Gundl asked him if he could shoot as well as he made coffee, he became distinctly less friendly. Swiss soldiers, he explained, were among the best in the world: they even took their rifles home with them and kept them in a cupboard there, always ready to hand. And he showed Gundl his rifle. On that same day she upset a Swiss woman badly, by innocently referring to the Rhône as a 'brook'.

When, at last, we came close to the Matterhorn, it towered to gigantic heights above us, with a banner of cloud flying from its summit.

We had never imagined it could be so high; and we felt like midgets.

We looked up from time to time at the great spike, at its cloud-banner. Did we really mean to go up there? Ought we not first try the gentler Breithorn?

A man with impressive yellow stockings was coming up the path from near-by Zermatt. By way of small-talk we told him, without any beating around the bush, what our plans were – and that we intended to stay at least a week or ten days. At which point he declared himself as the collector of the local 'Residence-tax'; and could he please have eight days' worth of it, on the spot . . .

'*Residence-Tax?*' Surely our ears were deceiving us – this must be some kind of mistake. We were living in a tent – not much 'residence' about that, surely? In any case, we didn't propose to pay a red cent of our precious money. Indignation, anger, heated argument followed on either side. Nothing would move the man with those jolly stockings. So, off the four of us marched to the police-station.

We consulted among ourselves – suppose the man was right? At the last moment I had a brain-wave. Very politely, we explained to the Police Inspector that it had all been a misunderstanding – true, we were going to spend a week near the Matterhorn, but on its Italian side. *This* was only a short staging-post on our way to the frontier . . .

The Collector looked murder at me. The last barrier was down. Then we proceeded – still on the Swiss side – up to the hut. How would we fare tomorrow, we wondered?

It was dark. Ahead of us we could see electric-torches winking. We could hear ice-axes clinking against rock. The shapes of towers in the ridge were silhouetted around us. Overhead, a gigantic dark mass bulked up – the summit.

The cold air was tense with expectation. We must be sure not to lose contact, in the darkness, with the guided parties in front. The three of us were climbing, roped together, up pitches and over shadowy blocks in the gloom. It wasn't particularly difficult, but a little complicated – and endlessly high. There, now we had lost contact, after all . . .

Daylight came. We were absolutely on our own. Friable slabs, brittle ledges, everything crumbling, crumbling. Were we still really on the right track, following scratch-marks? I had just jumped to safety from a stance that broke away beneath my feet. The blocks went crashing down into the depths . . . Gundl watched them with startled eyes. Erich shook his head – there goes another! This can't be the right way. Then we heard voices coming down from the right, higher up the ridge. Up that way, then – out on to the east face . . .

We were at 12,500 feet. There stood the Solvay Hut, an eagle's eyrie clinging to the edge of the rocks; a shelter should the weather change – but at present it was fine. We drew in deep breaths of the thin air of the four-thousanders for the first time – yes, it was rarer, and cleaner. We felt fine.

Over there, that white comb must be the Lyskamm. I remembered the 'Dachstein Priest's' lecture. That was the Weisshorn, and over there the Obergabelhorn, and there the Dent Blanche, and the cluster of Monte Rosa's five summits. How huge and lovely it all was, and how proud we were to be mounting higher and higher on 'our' Matterhorn and not on the gently-rounded Breithorn. Grey fog was slowly forming a cowl over the sharp outlines of our summit. It was noon. Another thousand feet to go. Then it was afternoon.

How far now? Everything was dim and grey around us. Everything fell away precipitously, like the pitch of a steep roof. Gasping for breath, we were now working our way up on all fours. We glanced timidly downwards, to the horrific abyss yawning below us – the North Face, directly under us.

The ridge flattened, the snow levelled off. Was that a cross over there? Ye sons of man, we were up! We were on top! On the summit ridge. A few yards more. We embraced, hugged each other, danced with joy. We had captured our Matterhorn – we three had done it!

True, we could see nothing, absolutely nothing – no mountains, no valleys – only one another, some rocks, some snow and a cross, ghostly in the fog. But it was the summit-cross on the Matterhorn.

The wind was howling round the Solvay Refuge, rattling its roof, tugging at its planks, in the night. We felt comfortable and safe, up there at 13,700 feet. Everything had gone smoothly on the descent, except for a mishap on the summit's steep roof, when Erich suddenly found himself hanging on one spike of his crampons and shortly afterwards landed on my shoulders after a short tumble. We looked down the abyss of the north face in terror. Fortunately, I was belayed.

Yes, we had been lucky. Our first four-thousander had entailed some risk, and we hardly knew enough to realize all the dangers involved. But when you are eighteen, you are inclined to go straight for what you want, without lengthy détours.

We lay there in the hut, too tired and happy to make any further plans. One thing was quite certain: this was not the last time we should be coming here.

What is it, then, that turns a dream into an aim? Just those little words: 'I want to.' Let us leave insuperable difficulties to those who believe such things exist.

For me, the Matterhorn was a giant's stride into the future. On it, I learned, for the first time, what one can achieve, if one really wants to.

One Step . . .

The old churchyard at Courmayeur is different from other churchyards; at least so it seems to me. The wooden war-crosses stand there like sinister birds of prey, with anonymous, white marble ones between. Mont Blanc and the Dent du Géant look down on it all.

Among those curious crosses stands one that doesn't seem to belong there at all – two simple wooden planks, cruciform. Yet it does belong there . . . Erich. He fell from the Dent du Géant.

Whenever Wolfi and I pass through Courmayeur, we usually go down to the old churchyard. Mostly we go separately, just as it happens to come into one or the other's mind. If I find a few wild-flowers there, I know Wolfi has been. Though it could have been the amiable, white-haired Headmistress of the kindergarten in Entrèves, just as well . . .

Four of us had come to Courmayeur together; all of us on our first visit. Mont Blanc towered gigantic over the green of the valley – almost 13,000 feet above us, draped in thin clouds, in banners of snow. We wheeled our push-bikes happily through the narrow alley-ways, watching the gaily-hued life of the place; buying a few trifles. Erich beamed through his glasses, his whole happy student-face alight with pleasure. 'My children,' he said, 'in a few days we shall be standing on that great mountain up there!' And he looked up at Mont Blanc, high over the roof-tops.

He had come with his Peilstein climbing-partner, Wolfgang Stefan, dark, slight, quiet, though sometimes very funny. He was a student too. They had been training hard recently and had reached a pretty high standard. I had Peter Heilmayer, from Salzburg, with me; he had not been climbing as long as the others, but he was keenness itself. We had all still to get used to the thin air, so we had decided not to make Mont Blanc our first objective.

The first thing we needed was a 'base camp'! We looked around for one, and in due course – in Italy anything can happen – found ourselves sitting in the middle of a kindergarten, cared for and cosseted, adulated and admired – talking broken Italian to the best of our ability. The Headmistress, a friendly old lady, saw to our every need; even the kitchen-staff was glad to take a look at, and to look after, some of these tough guys, who hang on ropes from icy walls, just in order – God knows why! – to climb some savage peak. We were, of course, delighted, explaining what we meant to do, letting them darn our socks, even allowing them – after a little hesitation – to wash our smalls. We tried to jodel, learned the '*Montanara*', sang the '*Bergvagabunden*' song to them, and the whole kindergarten then proceeded to serenade us with the '*chiesetta alpina*', which moved me (rapidly promoted to the status of professional photographer) to take a group picture. And, of course, we should be coming back to see them, year after year . . .

Erich was laughing and winking at me, as I had the whole kindergarten lined up in front of us, and unfolded my tripod with true professional skill; a real *fotografo* to the life, posing a few individual figures, with all the vision and assured hand-gestures of a true artist – until, finally, I pressed the shutter. We all laughed as I wiped my forehead with my Sunday-best handkerchief. It was all just too good to be true. Not in the wildest dreams of a mountaineer was there ever such a base camp, so many nice people all gathered in one spot!

We had decided to make the Dent du Géant our first climb. It is a savage rock-tooth, over 13,000 feet high. Well, actually, the figure is a little misleading, for it is the precise altitude reached by the summit. If you approach it by the normal route, all you have to do is less than 3,000 feet of steep but easy snow and rock, to the actual foot of the Tooth itself. Then there is only 700 feet of real climbing, to get to the top. No easy climbing this – Grade III – but we knew there were fixed ropes. We had been told how fearfully airy the climb was; when you clung to the front face of the needle, there was nothing but 3,000 feet or more of thin air under the soles of your boots.

We crossed the bergschrund, and I roped up with Peter, the least experienced member of the party.

'Aren't you going to rope up too?' I asked the others.

'We've got crampons – we'll get along all right.'

They certainly were getting along all right, obviously in tremendous form. Soon they were up there, on the '*Gengiva*', the 'Gum', at the foot of the Tooth itself, where they had agreed to wait for us.

Our successive rope's-lengths ran out; time moved leisurely by. At last we reached the ridge, close to the huge tower, with its vertical walls of reddish-brown granite. Over there, Wolfi and Erich were traversing the sloping snow-field of the '*Gengiva*'. Then . . . Erich slipped . . . threw himself face-down on his axe, braking his slide . . . but, no! . . . he went on sliding . . . Why, in heaven's name, didn't the axe grip? . . . went on sliding . . . sliding . . . sliding . . . out of sight . . .

Wolfi was standing there, shattered, struck dumb. We rushed across to him, arrived breathless. Quick! There was nothing to be seen, but possibly . . . Quick! Wolfi was lowering me on the rope.

There was a score in the snow . . . where he had tried to get a hold with his hands . . . then a couple of rocks – could he have grabbed them? We shouted: silence from the great white abyss. Could he be hanging, caught up in those rocks, having somehow got a grip, somewhere? Unconscious . . .?

Or? Too horrible to contemplate. It *mustn't* have happened!

The farther I moved down that white surface on the rope – it soon became a sheer gully – the more sure I was of the dreadful truth. It was hard, bone-hard down here, not a chance of checking one's fall, nothing to get a hold on, nothing but a slide at increasing speed.

They added another rope, and I reached the rocks. Nothing . . . no Erich . . . nowhere . . . no answer from the bottomless depths. It had really happened.

Wolfi saw me safely up on the rope, threw me a questioning glance. I looked at him, and he knew.

If we came up from the bottom, we should find him – or would we? He might be lying on the top of a pillar, or in a crevice in that 3,000-foot precipice; or even, over there, on the other side. Could he possibly be alive still? We hurried down the normal route, hoping for a miracle in which we no longer had any faith.

There was a party coming up. Had they seen or noticed anything? Heard anything? No, not a thing; had something happened, then? Yes, one of us had gone, fallen down the face. We left them standing there incredulous, and hurried on, down, down into those awful depths. We looked down on to an old cone of avalanche-snow, far, far down in a bay at the bottom of the face. We saw an elongated black stain on it. Could it be Erich? That kind of snow is not as hard as rock; he might have been lucky – Dear God, grant he had had luck, like Payer when he fell on the Ortler! – but then, of course, it might not be Erich, after all.

We raced down, panting for breath, never seeming to get any nearer. It was a long, long way down – we had already been more than an hour. The stain was the shape of a man. It didn't move. Could be . . .

No way down, here – everything fell away savagely into a hollow, more than a thousand feet, below us. We should have to come round from outside and below, skirting the base of the wall.

There was that dark thing down there on the snow – probably Erich. Nearly 3,000 feet below the '*Gengiva*'. Dear God!

We circled round the base of the rocks, crossing level snow towards the hollow, where the avalanche-cone gradually came into view.

Wolfi ran on ahead up the last 300 feet – I was past following, my knees had gone soft on me. Yes, that bundle up there was a man, was Erich, motionless on the bloodstained snow. Wolfi had reached it. And there he stood, just stood.

At last I arrived. Yes, it was he; his anorak, the grey rift, the . . .

There was a cry in the silence.

It was Erich, his face shockingly disfigured. Wolfi was still standing there, dumb, motionless. I watched the tears running down his face.

That afternoon, we brought him down to Entrèves. Once again he lay in the triangular tent we had used on the Matterhorn. Then we placed him on a bier in the little chapel, over whose slate roof we had looked up at Mont Blanc a few days before.

What was the point of it all —?

We held a vigil over our dead all through the night. I had never seen the stars so big as they were that night; they flickered as though a storm were passing over Heaven itself. Inexplicable.

And most inexplicable of all – there were voices in the air.

Neither Wolfi nor I could give it up. For us the mountains meant everything, as they had for Erich. Not even his death could alter that. Only Peter gave up climbing, later on. Of course we had to ask ourselves whether falling stones, avalanches, a disintegrating hold might not one day dictate an end to it all, however much care we exerted? Could be − but we said 'no' and took great precautions with our belaying. Wolfi and I went climbing together more and more, we were ideally matched, and we became a rope of two − a rope of two equal partners, Diemberger-Stefan or Stefan-Diemberger, each capable of leading it, equally capable of acting as second, according to circumstances. Mostly we led turn and turn about, for our understanding was complete.

Naturally, that did not all come about in a single day. Every mountaineer knows that a real rope partnership is a kind of communal life, in which complete mutual confidence has to be built up. For when one partner, in full knowledge of his own competence, caution or courage, decides to make a move, to use a piton or not, to give up or to go on − his decision absolutely involves the life of the other, bound to him by the same rope. One does not forget that.

One thing is indisputable: everyone you knot-up on a rope with you is different, and on the mountains you will learn to know him. For they reveal each man for what he is.

Without our meticulous and iron-hard training in climbing techniques on Vienna's Peilstein, Wolfi and I could hardly be alive today, after the countless climbs we have done together. And, in spite of everything, it must be admitted that once or twice we both owed our survival to our lucky stars, or to the other's skill. The summer climbing seasons which ensued were long ones: during one, we climbed twenty-five four-thousanders, including some great traverses; the next took us from the Wilde Kaiser to the Bregaglia, on to Mont Blanc, back to the Valais and finally to the Brenta Dolomites. Gradually we grew more and more at home in the whole great sweep of the Alps between Vienna and Marseilles. Then I, too, began to live the greater part of the year in the city of two million inhabitants, which was Wolfi's birthplace.

Fortunately, the Alps begin on its doorstep, in the Wienerwald.

Book-keeping and Pull-ups

Post-war Vienna. From the 'Piaristenkeller' rises the theme-song of 'The Third Man'; the town is punctuated by Russians and Americans, with a few British and French thrown in. Everyone is on his best behaviour, and fraternizes; we have been 'liberated', but unfortunately we are 'occupied'. Some years were still to roll by before Austrian *laissez faire* and Russian Vodka would combine to negotiate a bilateral agreement. 'But,' said the Viennese, 'we'll live it out!'

Early each morning, with a thunderous roar, the No 13 came rolling along the Piaristengasse, in District 8; faded-red, ancient and rust-covered – the tram. Later, at regular intervals, right through till the evening. When it came, the peace of the Alley, in which passers-by and pigeons promenaded happily, for few motor-cars used it, was rudely shattered. And every time No 13, having completed its approach-run the length of the straight road, took the bend opposite the Tröpferlbad, the air was rent by martial sounds – a squealing, a howling, a grating cacophony, which penetrated the topmost storeys as well as the deepest cellars. However, Frau Sedlacek and Herr Navratil, on the ground floor, both dismissed it with the same casual acceptance. 'Only the No 13.' they thought; for the Viennese can get used to anything.

Indeed, No 13 belonged to the very life and being of that thorough-fare. Only the tram-driver registered a protest every morning against his miserable lot. Since I lived directly above the bend, I was able to observe how he deliberately took a run, the whole length of the Piaristengasse, so that he could thunder into the curve with the greatest possible momentum: there could be no doubt that it was done on purpose. Did he want to arouse the conscience of the world? Because he was unhappy with his job? Had he got a grudge against the bend? Or did he simply want to wake us to a new day?

The rails had to be replaced every six months. Fortunately for us, No 13 did not run at night. All the same, it was cruelly early in the morning when it thundered past my window for the first time each day, to be followed immediately by that marrow-shattering screech. Then the Piaristengasse was wide awake. So was I . . .

Surely the man hadn't really meant to be a tram-driver at all; he must have had something quite different in mind?

And that thought brought back to my mind my pages of book-keeping material . . .

What was to become of me – me, the crystal-hunter, the cyclist, the embryo climber? I knew one could achieve anything one really wanted to – but what was I to want? There was no career to fit me.

If all the millions I was transferring from one account to another were really mine, I knew well enough what my goal would be: Exploration . . . Voyages of discovery . . .

There were Sven Hedin and Heinrich Harrer, for instance; how had they managed it? Riches would be the solution but – by Columbus, as I broke an egg into the frying-pan on the electric cooker! – reality was very different. These were the facts of life: a remote back-room in a students' hostel in the Piaristengasse – forty schillings a month, three beds, three chests and a heating-stove that didn't work. There the three of us sat, opposite each other, warmly-clad against the cold, in fleece-jackets, sheepskins and a couple of blankets round our shoulders – the ex-commando parachutist from the North Africa front, now turned sculptor; a book-keeper who would not be finished with his exams for years, though he was fully competent; and I. Our way of life was rather like that of an expedition's base camp; and female visitors were taboo. (According to the latest reports the ladies of Vienna later occupied the hostel by way of a protest: but not in our time.) The parachutist-sculptor carved religious statues; as he said, you have to earn a living somehow. And then, for his own amusement, he made the most wonderful drawings.

As for me, in spite of everything, I had discovered my own little America, one I could manage – the Peilstein in the Wienerwald – that climbers' practice-ground, with its innumerable crannies and climbs. Back there again tomorrow on my bike! According to the Peilstein Song:

> 'There's fever and fun, and the boys and the girls
> Climbing the rocks like flies up a wall;
> And if, in their sport, should one of them fall . . .'

No, no falling for me, thank you; the one taste of it, recently, had been quite enough of a good thing. Railli, supposed to be belaying me, had taken a beautiful header into thin air; however, the piton had held. Now, let's see how fit I am. Twenty – yes, really, twenty – pull-ups on the door-frame! What do I care about non-existent millions in an account-book?

I wondered whether the Career-Consultant, who turned up one day at the Graduation-class, was right: he said I hadn't a hope. After I had filled up the questionnaire ('Would you sooner be a chimney-sweep or a dentist?') with meticulous care, to the great delight of the class, I developed the curved line on a test-sheet, not into a little sponge or even an umbrella, but into a caricature of our Careerist – complete with three tiny hairs on his bald cranium. Not even a staggering likeness between the test-line and that refulgent dome could persuade him that I had great talent. (God is just: and I too count my ultimate blessings.)

And what else didn't I do? I spent six months intoning, in a bass voice, Schubert's songs and Sarastro, to please the lady who taught me singing and was certain that I was a great 'find', for whom she prophesied a splendid future. Vowel-production: 'The rain in Spain falls mainly on the plain' . . . six months of it. Then I rejected other heavier precipitation on the more level parts of Iberia because they told me to give up climbing, for the good of my voice. And Sarastro was converted to mountain-gypsy tunes on the guitar.

What about rocks? A career as a mining-engineer? I left Leoben in a hurry at the end of a single term. Was I to spend the whole of my life sitting near a mine? Quite impossible. Geology? No future in that, they told me in Vienna, at the time. I hesitated and made a big mistake, by not taking up Geology. Business? Not exactly exciting. But business-instructors were always wanted, and teaching was a family tradition. So I would be a business-instructor – that would at least give me time for the mountains. In four years I should have my University of Commerce diploma – and only then could I start to pass the special exams for being a teacher.

Four years sitting in a fleece-jacket in an unheated room in Vienna were undoubtedly good training for the icy giants of the Western Alps. Likewise the pull-ups on the frame of the door . . .

And then, the Peilstein. First with Railli, then with Wolfi, year in, year out, I was always to be found in that exciting realm of smooth towers and walls of superb grey limestone. There, right in the middle of the Wienerwald, amid the first fresh green of early spring on the trees – at first furtively making my trembling way up a Grade IV climb, complaining about one's 'in-and-out' form in April – but happier when I noticed the chap over yonder, who still had that 'sewing-machine' shake in his legs – right through to all the little masterpieces of technique, high above the trees aflame with autumn colours.

In between lay our great summer seasons – the Dolomites, the Bregaglia, Mont Blanc. In the autumn we all met again, around camp-fires or at huts, and told each other what great rock-faces we had 'taken apart' – thanks to our iron apprenticeship in the Peilstein school.

Yes, we formed a colourful, venturesome guild, we Peilstein-climbers who, Sunday after Sunday, turned up there from Vienna, twenty-five miles away, on our bicycles – till one or other of us filled everyone else with envy by acquiring a 'machine'. Full of relevant humour, too. One loft traverse high above the tree tops was embellished with a tram-car notice, in black-and-white enamel, which read: 'DON'T LEAN OUT.' And, for occasions when, accompanied by good advice from Wienerwald visitors, spiritually involved in our climbing ('there's a hand-hold, up to the right above you – about seven feet!'), one had safely mastered a difficult overhang and was clinging to nothing more than a few rugo-sities, 150 feet above the base of the climb, one was greeted by a dentist's placard: 'DON'T SPIT ON THE FLOOR!' Some of the names were very apt, too: you could take your pick from 'Suicide Crack' to 'Poster Pillar'. The rules, though unwritten, of the Peilstein fraternity were strictly observed. The novice started with the 'Balloon' scramble or 'The Slab'; our fair Viennese 'Mizzis' were put on to the easy but deep Schindeltal Chimney. And one universal rule: woe to him who used a piton on a 'free' climb! The unimaginable creature who started knock-ing his hooks into the superb hand-holds of the almost vertical 'Vegetar-ian's Arête' – the origin of the name remains obscure for, though the Peilstein brigade like potato salad, their diet is not exactly meatless – sparked off a minor revolution. From the Jahrerkanzel flowed sounds of local vernacular, boos rose from the Couloirs, loud echoes of rage rang from 'Monte Cimone' to the 'Matterhorn', and the sound of many angry voices floated across even to the distant 'Zinnen'; for the Peilsteiners can conceive of no greater crime than to bang a piton into the holds of that arête. Terrified, the ironmonger took to flight (He came, he 'nailed' in the wrong place, and was no more seen). Even so do the Peilsteiners protect the purity of their rocks!

One evening I was poring over my balance-sheets, while the sculptor was at his work close by. Presently he plucked at my sleeve and said: 'Come with me, I want to show you something.' He led me to the win-dow above the dark courtyard: 'Something quite unusual,' he declared, staring raptly up at the nocturnal skies. 'Look!' he said, pointing to a dazzling bright star, 'that's Venus; and the one quite close to it, the pale red one, that's Mars. It is very rare to see them in conjunction.' The two utterly different stars blinked; the one a bluish white, the other emitting occasional flashes of red – a magic spectacle. And then Kloska,

63

the sculptor, began to tell me about the nights, out in the Sahara, under the vast vault of the desert sky.

He told me, too, about the telescope mirror he wanted to make . . . I remembered a dusty old telescope and microscope lying unused in Salzburg. Suppose we put them together? We did, and it worked. Now we could see Saturn's ring, Jupiter's moons, Andromeda's gorgeous veil of vapours. Kloska, the parachutist in Rommel's army, the sculptor who carved holy figures and drew so beautifully, the human being who pursued his own quiet life and lived only for his art, was completely at home in the depths of the starlit sky, and now he initiated me into its mysteries. I knew nothing of his life, about which he rarely spoke. But one day he told me, as we were once again exploring the heavens, with that very special gift he had of contented relaxation, that the middle star in Orion's belt was not a star at all, but an indescribably distant cloud of shining vapour, which only looked like a star to the naked eye.

I trained the telescope on that tiny point of light, and saw a marvellous feathery, shimmering cloud . . .

'Its light takes ten years to get across from one end to the other of that cloud,' said Kloska.

And then I understood the peace which radiated from him.

Two on a Rope

We had got into a nice mess, damnation take it – properly sewn-up and stuck! There we were, hanging like flies on the three-thousand-foot face of the Croz dell' Altissimo, in the Brenta Dolomites, and nothing made sense any more. Everything was inimical, resistant, grey, smooth, unclimbable and repulsive: below me, a bottomless abyss . . .

The face of the Croz dell' Altissimo is the highest in the Brenta, carved as if by a knife out of a mountain accessible, on its other side, to sheep. It forms the lateral wall of a deep gorge. And there, halfway up it, were Wolfi and I, armed with a route-description in good clear Italian; our 'rock-sense' would, we said, make up for the bits we didn't understand, but since the last passage dictated by that rock-sense, it had all become Greek to us. No, not all: it 'strapiombed' everywhere, which meant it overhung. We had found the start of the route easily enough – a ledge with *mughi*, which assuredly meant little bumps, in it (a striking analogy with our Viennese 'Mugl'); since then it had 'placcted', vertically, 'strapiombed', over us, and 'fissured' – cracked or split – all around. And for the last hour I had had a nasty feeling that the description and the route no longer corresponded. At least, so my 'rock-sense' told me.

Suddenly, the coin dropped. That rusty piton at the adjectival pitch down below there had lured us on to the wrong traverse. It hadn't been the right adjectival pitch – the right one was much higher up. What kind of an adjectival pitch would that be, we wondered? Now it all depended on our 'rock-sense'!

So, now: straight on up, on barely recognizable holds, but fearfully smooth stuff. I banged a piton obliquely into a flake – it wouldn't hold a thing – so, on and up. At last I came to a minute ledge, which might provide a stance. I glued my face against the wall and hammered in another piton. It held!

Wolfi was coming up – clear of the airy slab, like a spider. It looked bizarre; the dark greenish-grey pattern of the wooded gorge, two thousand feet below, straight under his heels and above his shoulders.

'Watch out for that flake!'

65

'Yes, but the piton —'

Clatteration! Hold him, you've got to hold him! Agony in my knees, the rope cutting my shoulders, Wolfi's brown shock of hair twirling below me in mid-air, his body out over nothingness . . . You've got to hold him! I gritted my teeth, while he paddled in the air with his hands, feeling for the rock, finally got a hand-hold . . . – and that took his weight off my shoulders at last. I drew a deep breath; thanks be, the belaying-piton had held firm . . . but for the moment my tail was well down . . . we hung there on the stance for a few minutes. Then Wolfi led on up.

We did a climb every day. The glowing yellow east face of the Cima di Brenta, the enormous ice-packed chimney of the Cima degli Armi, the stratified mass of the Torre di Brenta, the soaring Campanile Alto, the magnificent rock-pillar of the 'Guglia'. Then more climbs: up the giant staircase of the Brenta Alta's south ridge, the three-thousand-foot arête of the Crozzon – airy routes in a realm of black-and-yellow rock-castles, high above the green carpet of meadows at their feet. We had got used to it; it no longer surprised us to find only a piton or two on vertical faces several hundred feet high; we had got to know the Brenta's rock, with its thousand rough wrinkles, bollards, spikes – often so needle-sharp that they hurt one's fingers – its caves and its 'hour-glasses', behind which one could thread a rope-sling: this peculiar Dolomite, whose amazing horizontal holds demanded great finger-strength. We could smile, now, at our rock-sense of the Croz dell' Altissimo; though we did pursue one more 'Via Fantasia' on the Torre di Brenta.

That same day, on ground not far from the base of the rocks, I found a Roman coin. Had it belonged to a soldier? Or to a hunter? For how long have men climbed up into the mountains?

All that was missing was a Grade VI climb. Cesare Maestri, 'the king of the Brenta', directed us to the Cima d'Ambiez: there was quite a pitch low down on it, he told us – the rest was a dream of a climb. That *was* a rock, a proper rock, he explained, his face lighting up with enthusiasm.

The evening before the climb: the whole face a dim blue shadowy thing, full of questions and surmises. Next morning, 1,200 feet of vertical cliff, brownish-red in the bright sunshine, riddled with holes and crannies. There were coffer-like overhangs, then a crack . . . I gasped for breath, spreadeagled on tiny protuberances; moved up a little and threaded through a piton; up again by a series of split-second decisions; worked my way farther up the face, which did its best to push me out and off – found a stance where I could take a breather. It was a gigantic free-climbing pitch, then; I wonder whether it still is?

Then followed the dream of a rock-climb, vertical, overhanging, pitonless, with innumerable small holes and wrinkles – perfect free-climbing on a sheer wall, with an infinity of air around us. At such moments you are gloriously conscious of your fingers, your muscles; of the toes of your boots winning a hold on the rough Brenta rock; of the wall, close to your face, shining black, brown and bright ochre amid the grey – like flower-patterns in a carpet – and all of it high above the combe down there at the foot of the climb. You are enmeshed in a bright web of thoughts, on which you climb ever higher, pulling yourself upwards from hand-hold to hand-hold, foot-hold to foot-hold, towards an ever-increasing freedom, while everything below you falls away – as you exalt yourself all the time.

Down there at the bottom, you see the shadows of the towers lengthen, and feel that you belong to your mountain with every fibre of your being and yet, at the same time, here, high above the abyss, utterly free of mind and spirit, you are acutely aware that you have arms and legs – and a body able to waft you upwards, because you have learned to overcome fear.

I belayed Wolfi up to a stance. We hardly spoke, we just climbed. Occasionally one of us remarked how splendid it was, and how right Cesare's assessment of the climb. I leaned my forehead against the rock; it was sunny and warm. What a joy, what a gift of fortune, it was to climb, to be alive in this lovely world! The very rock in front of me seemed a living thing.

A box of colour-slides. People coming, after their day's work, people who had perhaps a fortnight or three weeks' leave in a year, people who loved the mountains just as much as we did, many of whom the war had robbed of their best days . . . I was giving one of my first lectures. All of a sudden I myself was lost in it all, back in the middle of a summer spent between Mont Blanc and the Drei Zinnen. Everything else was forgotten.

We were at our 'base camp' in the Bregaglia. There were a couple of tents, socks flapping from the rope as they dried in the breeze, flocks of sheep in the distance, 'Peilstein-Joschi' snoozing on the 'post-prandial slab', Friedl sticking some plaster on finger-tips worn raw by climbing, Wolfi immersed in contemplation of the great blue face of Piz Badile, Hilde washing yet more socks in the mountain torrent. Here were to be found the loveliest camping-sites in the world; the most magnificent arêtes; and the worst-behaved sheep. Only yesterday they had devoured some of our savoury West-Alpine socks – one couldn't help laughing,

much as the climbers sympathized with the sorely-tried washer-woman:
climbing-socks, no mountain stream clear enough to wash them clean,
and no representative of the Society for Prevention of Cruelty to Ani-
mals within miles!

For a moment I was back in the lecture-room, then I was perched
once more two thousand feet above a glacier. 'Come up!' A lay-back up
a 'Piaz'-crack. 'You're there!' A still finer lay-back. 'And now it's my
turn!' Sunshine, clouds, the Cengalo Arête, with the smooth face of the
Badile opposite. Every climber knows that 'Bregaglia' is synonymous
with 'Bregaglia granite'. Fantastic rock-forms, incredibly sheer peaks,
carved by thousands of years out of the living rock, like monsters in the
grey dawn of history, with yellow and black lichens on their rough surfaces, towers, thin sword-blades of rock, spear-heads the size of a house,
the smooth flat scoop of a shovel nearly 3,000 feet high – the Badile
itself. And next to it the perfect, regular, gigantic curvature of the
Cengalo's outline, loftier still by a few hundred feet, raking the sky. The
thousand-foot 'Flat-iron', too, complete with hand-holds. Arêtes, arêtes
and more arêtes . . .

Wolfi and I did them all, on alternate days, including the Sciora di
Fuori and – it goes without saying – the towering North-east Face of the
Badile (I had already done that climber's dream, its arête). Then we
rode over to the Dolomites, with the Busazza Arête in the Civetta group
as our target; but when we got there – once again, needless to say – in
spite of our thirst for great ridge-climbs, we went straight up the north-
west face of the Civetta herself, the queen of all Dolomite face-climbs,
that glowing red screen of organ-pipes; soaring high above a southern
valley, which a boy with a bicycle had discovered years before.

How many life-times do we need to make all our dreams come true?

And now the 'Spigolo Giallo' and all the face-climbs on the Zinnen!
But when we arrived at the Paternsattel with our last few hellers in our
pockets, it rained. We bivouacked in a concrete hut, and sat on our
rucksacks, looking at each other, for three days. Then it started to snow.

Autumn had set in. There was nothing for it but to go home.

We always routed our long summer months in the Western Alps from
west to east, starting 'over there' in July and finishing up 'over here' in
the Dolomites by September. In the end we grew tired of bicycling;
hitch-hiking was far more comfortable. Finally, Wolfi acquired a small
motor-cycle, by dint of hard saving and, indeed, at the expense of our
basic principle not to lose a day of our treasured summer-forays into the
mountains by doing a single extra day's work. If it meant living on
porridge, it also meant more summits. Meanwhile, I had discovered the

'Grants for Important Ascents', earned lecture-fees, and paid regular visits to my generous 'Aunt Betty'. So yet another Alpine summer was assured.

We were at the start of the south face of the Dent du Géant – a rash of carabiners, the jingle of pitons, rope-slings for the feet, sunshine; and above us the vertical granite wall, with its overhangs.

I started up the first few feet, with a view to reaching the lowest piton, climbing 'free'. Hell, how the thing overhung! . . . No use . . . I had to come down again. Suddenly I heard a voice, saying in broken German: 'You should put a starting-piton in – it's the drill here. That one up there is the second one.'

A hop-pole of a long Frenchman had arrived at the starting-point, accompanied by a small fat one, and was quietly unpacking his snack-lunch. 'Thanks!' I growled at him, and started up again, ignoring his advice. Nice chap, behaving as if he owned the place – but we would show him! Up I went to within six inches, three inches, of that piton. Blast everything! I had to come down again. There I stood, panting, getting my strength back – I had put everything I had into it, that second time. Wolfi wrinkled his forehead; angrily, I banged in the piton in question; the long slab of a Frenchman sat quietly munching his sandwich. I knew I had seen that type with a woolly cap somewhere before. Never mind that . . . off I went, not exactly stylishly, but moving quickly – now we would get clear of the two sandwich-munchers!

I found a stance on an airy pulpit. 'Up you come!' I shouted down, to Wolfi, out of sight. The rope told me how smoothly and swiftly he was coming up; I could see his brown mop appearing around the corner, and – by Friday the thirteenth! – a woolly cap, too. That long slab had arrived at the same time, and was laughing, between a fine set of teeth: '*Alors*, the piton was all right, wasn't it?' – so paternal! – 'You see, I know my way about here; this is the seventh time I've done it.' *Seventh time!* He hauled in his rope – we were hanging out into thin air from that pulpit in all directions – and once again those teeth flashed above a tough chin. 'You don't mind if I go on ahead?' he asked. 'By the way – may I introduce myself? I'm Rébuffat . . .' So it was Gaston Rébuffat, the world-famous climber – admittedly the king of the castle in his Mont Blanc group: why, he must know every hold in it! Humbly, we mumbled our names, shook him by the hand – clinging with the other to the rock; then we leaned out even farther into the air to let him pass. Down below us the ropes swung slowly too and fro. Certainly an odd place for such an introduction.

For a while our human bunch of grapes – we were now four – hung out from the sun-baked face, nearly thirteen thousand feet up; then elegant French *étriers* jingled in space and Rébuffat disappeared from sight above an overhang.

A storm was raging on the Peuteret ridge – the weather had broken suddenly. We knew how many had died on the White Mountain, thirty to forty in some seasons – and how often the weather had been responsible for their failing to return from the peaks and faces of the massif.

Snow, and more snow – we had to get down before it was too late. We only had two days' provisions left, a stupid mistake. We groped our way down the Couloir, then through the ice-towers of the Fresnay glacier, valleywards. At last we were down safely, though minus our Peuteret ridge; but we had at least the turreted south ridge of the Aiguille Noire to show for it.

This damned weather! We had lived up there for a fortnight in the bivouac-box under the sharp tooth of the Fourche de la Brenva, before we could finally do the Arête du Diable on the Tacul and the south face of the Dent du Géant . . .

Every day, as we sat there, the gigantic White Brenva face had shimmered down on us, mostly out of the clouds; and the north face of the Aiguille Blanche de Peuteret, with the ice-avalanches roaring down it to shatter the silence.

A thought entered our minds: it must be marvellous to climb those white walls, that difficult ice – those unique ice-faces, huge, forbidding, holdlessly smooth, with their blue bulges, their crystalline towers. For, although we were already committed to rock of every grade of difficulty, we had not yet taken a single step in the world of cold, ice-armoured faces.

Was there something keeping us away? Was rock-climbing to be our whole life? Or was the other thing just something which would come in good time?

When I look back today, the following thoughts spring to my mind: Wolfi had come to the mountains from an apprenticeship on rock, I, who had started as a crystal-hunter, from the white world of snow. All the same, once the day dawned when to climb a peak by the normal route, or in the course of a long traverse, failed any longer to satisfy, I had become a rock-climber, like Wolfi. Rock – with all the difficulties of extreme climbing – that was the thing: cliffs, ridges, arêtes of rock.

Now, in our third Alpine season, we both thought for the first time about an ice-climb: the Brenva face of Mont Blanc. The thought was stifled by masses of snow, falling day after day. Our first intrusion into the world of ice-climbs, into the realm of mountaineering of every grade of difficulty in the white element – never of course, to the exclusion of rock-climbing – would have to wait till next summer.

This process of development in the whole wide field of Alpinism over a lifetime will doubtless repeat itself for many a climber. There is a biological parallel here: in the grey prehistoric days, we all swung from branch to branch. The laws of heredity have repeated the process in our own day. The development is simply that the naked 'hairy ape' has at last invaded the ice-world.

'The standard of a nation's cultural development is recognizable by its table-manners', I read on the page of newspaper in which I had wrapped our tomatoes. Well, well! And we Austrians are supposed to be civilized people. Yet, there, opposite me, Wolfi was sitting on the grass, barefoot, cooking polenta. Were we really a good advertisement for our country? At that moment Wolfi pushed a tomato into his mouth and for several minutes gave a good impersonation of someone trying to swallow a tennis-ball.

'Have you ever considered,' I ask him, 'what kind of an impression of Austria we present when we are abroad?'

Wolfi made a puzzled internal noise corresponding to '*mmmmmh*', the expression in his eyes exactly matching the tennis-ball in his mouth. Then, after swallowing: 'What's wrong with it?' he enquired.

'This paper says you can recognize the standard of a nation's cultural development by its table-manners,' I explained, looking pointedly at the tomatoes. Wolfi laughed, picked another one out of the paper and shoved it into his mouth. It appeared that the recognition of cultural standards lay behind the next tomato. I gave up my attempts at education, fetched my spoon out of my trouser-pocket and immersed myself in polenta. Wolfi did likewise – it is just one of those freaks of chance: he is left-handed, I am right-handed, so we can spoon things out of the same pot at the same time. (This is known as rationalization: arriving at an end by the simplest means.) Anyway, we only had one pot. Wolfi put a finger in his mouth and cleaned his teeth. 'You should use a toothpick,' I reminded him, licking my spoon clean, 'and do it in the loo! You aren't civilized.' (A bronze-coloured millepede was climbing over the polenta-bag.) Wolfi spat scornfully: 'That I suppose is why I developed the system for making do with only one cooking-pot – and with no need for washing up, at that?' (Sequence: polenta or porridge, then a soup-cube, finally tea – and then turn the pot upside down and leave it in the sun.) 'Any objections?'

'None,' I admitted, having exhausted all my arguments. After all, inventive powers are part of civilization, too.

Wolfi looked at me pensively and fired his final shot: 'This seems to be your day for moralizing. Do you know, it's a long time since you trimmed the ragged edges of the holes in your trousers – shall I lend you my knife?'

I did not reply, but, using a piece of newspaper for a napkin, wiped my mouth and raised the aluminium saucer of tea to my lips. After all one must start from small beginnings, and good intentions have their value. See! Wolfi was following my example . . .!

Of the newspaper, there was nothing left.

20,000 Feet in Twenty-four Hours

Had we been seized by some form of madness? Or had we joined the tribe of mere record-hunters? No: we were simply itching to know whether we had the necessary stamina to climb the Obergabelhorn with its crystal-white north face, so difficult of access – as it were, in the original conditions, before there were any club huts – direct from the valley-level.

We were in splendid shape. After various other climbs, we had just done the 4,000-foot north face of the Dent d'Hérens in eight hours. What a gem of an ice-chimney – the crucial key-pitch of the Welzenbach route (how often had it been borne in on us that the name of that great ice-expert stood for climbs of exceptional beauty of form and quality)!

Our fourth and fifth summer seasons in the Western Alps had afforded us an initiation into this new realm of the great ice-faces. We had savoured the crystalline element, in various degrees of steepness and severity, on the Dent d'Hérens, the Obergabelhorn, Breithorn, Lyskamm, Aiguille Blanche and Grands Charmoz; and finally the great Brenva face of Mont Blanc. On our way to the gigantic north face of the Dent d'Hérens, we had cast longing eyes up at one of the greatest 'combined' rock and ice-climbs in the Alps – the north face of the Matterhorn. We had both got over the days of our rock-climbing intoxication in the Brenta Dolomites; we knew now that one could not do everything. Whether on rock or on ice, our minds were turning more and more to the really big climbs. If the actual climbing was less attractive than on many a smaller peak, we now found the very size of the undertaking more impressive and exciting.

20,000 feet without a break: from our tent outside Steinauer's shack at Winkelmatten, near Zermatt, to the top of the 13,365-foot Obergabelhorn, and back down again to our tent. In between lay various ascents and descents; the climax, of course, being the mountain's delicately ribbed North-west Face, an ice-wall whose base is so difficult to approach that, to the best of our knowledge, it had only been climbed five times. Each party had tried to reach its foot, which rises from a savage glacier-cauldron, by a different route. One of them had actually climbed *down* a ridge from the summit in order to get there. And we, starting out from Zermatt, had somehow to find a way over the high intervening range of rock to the west, so as to get down into the cauldron beyond it. Once there, the face is a smooth, finely-drawn slope with an inclination of 55 degrees. The whole thing would normally take three days.

One o'clock in the morning. We fastened the tent-door behind us and left Winkelmatten, its huts shadowy shapes in the moonlight. We went up into the night, past the benches thoughtfully placed by the Tourist Board between the dark trunks of the pines, past the sleeping steinbocks in their enclosure.

By dawn we had negotiated the boulders of the moraine and reached the Rothorn Hut, at 10,500 feet, having come up fully 5,000 feet. The sky was an extraordinary apple-green, above the pale glimmer of the Wellenkuppe's snow-cap. We felt marvellous, and stopped for a cup of tea before continuing the ascent.

The sun came up, painting the rocks a reddish-brown. Our breath turned to a vapour-cloud. What a glorious day this was! Over there rose the Triftjoch, a rocky saddle high above the glacier, our next objective. Up here there was a great deal of fresh snow. The question was whether we should be able to get down from the saddle into that cauldron of ice lying in the valley beyond it, and so reach the foot of our north face?

Nine o'clock, on the saddle . . . opposite us, the Obergabelhorn, shining like a crystal, seamed with bluish-white flutings, still a mile away beyond that deep and ice-filled glacier-bowl, involving a descent of hundreds of feet to its bed of green shadows, blue séracs, huge cre- vasses and – beyond all doubt – masses of freshly-fallen snow, promising much hard labour. The great white face of our peak flung back the light like a mirror, across the deep ice-blue of the dark network of rock-slopes below us on our side – a miracle of loveliness!

There was certainly no direct way over to it from here. Wolfi bit his lip, as he scanned the surging, long drawn-out corniced ridge to the left, the North-east Ridge of our four-thousander. Could we reach the foot of our face by following it, say, as far as the great *gendarme*, and then cutting diagonally downwards? A steep and most unusual route, surely involving the longest traverse we had ever met? But first we had to turn back and climb the Wellenkuppe.

· · · · ·

Late in the morning we were on the 12,796-foot summit of the Wellenkuppe, where the North-east Ridge of the Obergabelhorn begins – an undulating edge, swinging up above the abyss in a long curve, like some narrow suspension-bridge, to the sharp summit of the peak.

By midday we had got to the *gendarme,* and started on our diagonal downward traverse. God, how that slope went plummeting down!

We went on traversing diagonally downwards well into the afternoon, clinging to a 60 degree wall of ice for one hour, two hours; climbing like two tiny spiders across that huge white slope, traversing and traversing diagonally downwards . . .

At last, the bergschrund at the bottom lay only a rope's length below us. Who was going to climb down into it and up out of it again, for the sake of the record, to regularize our ascent of the face? You perhaps, Wolfi? No, not Wolfi. Perhaps you will oblige, Kurt? No, not Kurt . . . we decided that our climb would have to count without that small formality.

So, at last, we could start on our ascent of that enormous crystal, straight up the middle, from its base to its summit, up a face something like 500 yards high. It would be rather nice to have a camp-bed along for rests at the stances!

An endless succession of white ribs, sweeping upwards at 55 degrees, uniform, similar, symmetrical, regular . . . peaceful, and soothing to the mind . . . with a gossamer film of ice-dust rippling down over them.

It was a positive dream of loveliness. One of us moved up, belayed by the other; then the other one moved up, belayed in his turn. Our belaying pitons went in solidly at the stances.

Yes, a camp-bed would have been rather nice . . .

That went on for three hours. Overhead, the ridges were closing in to meet at the summit. Just below it, we were suddenly aware that we had defeated the crucial challenge of that vast white uniformity. Now, straight up and out by the *direttissima* (as a gesture)! Fearfully steep, absolutely smooth ice, with a 70 degree pitch, then a few rocks – and there we were, on our summit. So much for that!

We sat there for a quarter of an hour, while sun-shot mists drifted about us. It was a lovely world! It was also past four o'clock – fifteen hours since we had started out across the meadow down there in Zermatt. We had completed more than half our journey. Somehow, all sense of time seemed to have deserted us. There was the sun, of course, and our watches . . .

We were on our way down, moving steadily along that corniced

75

suspension-bridge of a ridge. Suddenly, the lower half of the Matterhorn's north face loomed out of the mists, glittering in a mantle of freshly-fallen snow. Before us rose our *gendarme,* with thick grey fog all around.

The fog turned yellow, and began to simmer. Light was coming through it – brighter and still brighter, finally dazzling. There was a stir in the air; then, as if by magic, the whole world lay clear. There stood the Dent Blanche and the Obergabelhorn, drenched in the liquid gold of the sunset. Everything was golden-yellow – the mists below us, the mountain-face, our tracks in the snow. The hours had suddenly dissipated into thin air. The sun was going down. We were tired and transfigured – we felt as if we could go on like this for ever. Everything about the day was odd – and now night was drawing in again.

7 p.m.: back at the Rothorn Hut, after eighteen hours and some 13,000 feet of up and down to plague our limbs. How pleasant it would be to stay here at a comfortable hut! Resisting the temptation, we staggered on down towards Zermatt – we *had* to know whether we could achieve the aim we had set ourselves. Boulders, the zig-zag path, darkness, thoughts – I never wanted to be on that mountain-face any more, all I wanted was to be in our tent: in Wolfi's Alpine-Association-Section-Austria double-lined tent, made of material tested in the Himalaya, which always let the rain in, because it doesn't rain in the Himalaya, it snows . . .

Wolfi had stopped. 'I'm waiting for the moon to come up,' he said, and lay down among the boulders. I was waiting for the next bench, above Zermatt, and went on my way towards it . . . *tarum-tumtum* . . . *tarum-tumtum* . . . *tarum tumtum* . . . *hoppla!*

There it was, my bench. Praise be to God and the Tourist Board. Now the moon could come up, if it wanted to.

A pretty young lady with an odd-looking handbag and stiletto-heeled-shoes was coming up the meadows towards me – a sight to cheer one: big almond-eyes, long, dark shining hair, slim legs. She sat down by me and opened her pretty mouth. 'Would you care to take me up with you to the Finch Terrace?' she enquired.

Would I, a guide in this year 2,000, care to – not likely! There was a batting of blue eyelashes. I thought it over: a promenade like that on a chilly ice-terrace? Hadn't people in this day and age anything better to think about, than that one-track North Face of the Dent d'Hérens?

Out loud, I said: 'The coffee isn't at all good up there and they haven't finished the surface-lighting of the crevasses. The kiosk over there on the Tyndall ridge serves a much better Mocca. Of course, we could just eat a Cassata and then climb a few feet, if you really want to;

or we could take the dear old lift to the summit – though I'm afraid it's a bit ancient now.' (Even in 2000 AD, a guide must show at once that he knows his area, if he expects further assignments.)

The sweet young lady got a mirror out of her handbag and redrew her mouth with a lipstick. 'What would you charge?' she asked.

'Hm!' I temporized. Dear old Fiechtl, in whose day everything was so simple, had been dead a long time. I rummaged between punched cards in my rucksack for the latest punched computer-card, which now takes into account, day by day, not only the temperature, air-pressure, wind-force and the state of the weather, but also the guide's fitness. (I had been relegated to Grade I – so many flights up to the terraces had properly grounded me; and all those summit-parties up to the new chapel on top of the Breithorn – these occupational hazards!) If Welzenbach only knew that nowadays one flies up to enjoy a small black coffee in the middle of his ice-wall . . .

But wait a moment; something very odd was happening. The lovely one was pulling an ice-piton out of her little bag, carabiners, rock-pitons and – by Fiechtl and Welzenbach! – a gossamer-thin storm-suit of the new Mars-tested super-skin. Surely she couldn't actually want to *climb* the old route up to the Terrace? Impossible . . . Kurt, pinch your arm, you must be dreaming . . .

I could hear someone running in the woods. Wolfi came past at a jogtrot. The moon was up, too. Down below, a few lights were winking – Zermatt. We stumped on down, and finally – 'by the skin of our teeth' – up the slope that rises to Winkelmatten.

At 1 a.m. we collapsed into the tent like two felled trees – almost exactly 24 hours after leaving it, and after 20,000 feet of height differential. (Later I worked it over again, and it proved to be only 19,300 feet. Nothing is ever complete, not even the most beautiful chapter-heading. We ought, after all, to have done that little extra bit down into the bottom of the bowl.)

We woke up at three o'clock the next afternoon and stretched ourselves in the sun outside the tent. Someone was coming up from Zermatt, through the meadows.

Yellow mists were still floating before my eyes – but now I was suddenly very wide awake. Yellow-stockings: the local collector of the 'residential tax', no doubt about it! I took one big leap into the tent, to resume my residence there. Wolfi continued to lie on the grass, smiling happily. Now for a local gala!

The tax-man arrived. Soon Wolfi was babbling amiably about the

77

Matterhorn and how long he and his buddy, asleep there in the tent, proposed to stay around that lovely mountain. It was quite a pleasure to listen to him, now he was coming to the point. 'In any case,' he said, making a significant pause – 'we're starting for the Theoduljoch today and going over on to the Italian side . . .'

Perhaps I had not quite slept off the effects of yesterday, but the yellow knee-hose seemed to change colour. I gave a loud yawn, opened the tent-flap and blinked at my old acquaintance. It was worth two whole days of residential tax. He actually recognized me.

We were sitting in the Hörnli Hut, filing the points of our crampons as sharp as possible, for the North Face. Old Kronigk, the hutkeeper, winked at us. He knew us by now and had guessed our intentions; but then he shook his head. 'The weather,' he said. It was beautifully sunny outside. We went on filing. Wolfi had just come back from a solo climb of the Zmutt ridge, from which he had taken a good look at the face. It was in excellent condition: this time we would do it.

By midnight a storm was raging and it was snowing hard – unbelievable masses of snow. Everything had turned white, and the warm wind was coming from the south-west. Not a hope, this time. Next year, perhaps.

Not long afterwards,we were pedalling, as so often before, out into the woods in their autumn glory, to the familiar grey walls and towers of our Peilstein practice-ground, where the local 'Matterhorn' and 'Monte Cimone' stand side by side. Wolfi had acquired a girl-friend. It was really charming to see how careful he was that she didn't fall off – how devotedly he showed her every hand- and foot-hold. But – thought I, what about . . .? Wolfi reassured me about my 'but': he would not let her come along on our next summer's north-face campaign, he promised.

I breathed again, rejoicing. That was how it should be! When one went to the mountains, one should think about mountains and nothing but the mountains. There spoke the true, the genuine mountaineer; he was one of the real ones – *un des purs*, as Samivel has called them. (Anyway, nothing to be surprised about; wasn't he my rope-mate?)

I, of course, had no idea then what fate had in store for me. I did not know that, next summer, I would continually be persuading Wolfi that we needed further supplies of fresh food for our ice-climbs; and that each time, as soon as he had blessed me resignedly with his agreement, I would be hurrying down hot-footed to Zermatt . . .

Just to fetch apples, of course.

Daisies, a cat and the North Face of the Matterhorn

'She loves me . . . she loves me not . . .'

Daisies on the North Face of the Matterhorn – on its stances?

Shining dark rock, blue glittering ice, light in the bursting bubbles of glassy mountain-waters – marsh-marigolds – veils of ice rippling down the face —

Rébuffat said it: 'A marvellous heap of stones, the Matterhorn.'

Sunshine on the North Face. Hot sun. Ice-blossoms, tinkling down from the rocks, out into the darkness of the valley, flashing yellow and white . . .

Daisies? Anything is possible – if one thinks of it.

Anything is possible, when a determined, resolute Swiss girl packs her bag and says: 'I've got a dog already – now I want a *husband*!' Especially if she knows where to find him: in Vienna. So she travels to Vienna.

Obviously, we Austrians must have a wonderful reputation in foreign parts as husbands; we are supposed to be faithful, reliable, happy-go-lucky, sociable, comfortable and hard-working; if we happen to be a bit slovenly, well, they hope that can always be cured.

I forgot a most important thing: love asks no questions. I asked questions: What is this that comes rolling down on me by Transalpine Express right across the Alps? Apart from what, why just on Vienna (fateful thought!)? I wonder what she looks like . . .?

Wolfi and I were on the Peilstein. 'Your mind doesn't seem to be on climbing today,' he suggested. No, I was thinking about quite a different matter.

It was in the Bernina, three years before. White peaks above the Tschierva Hut; the Biancograt, Piz Roseg opposite, Scerscen in between. Huge cascades of ice. But I, lying totally snow-blind in the darkened dormitory of the hut, could see none of these things. My fate arrived after a six-hour trek up the Rosegtal on pliant espadrilles, with blisters on her soles, gritted teeth, a hard head and a very sweet soul. She wanted, for once, to see the homeland peaks from near by – not only the distant lands in the wide, wide North.

Grit under my eyelids. Dark, confused contours. My lids felt swollen, and now and then came stabbing pain. Damn it, don't rub them! Hardly able to open my eyes, I lay quietly . . . waiting . . . in the darkness . . .

That was the door . . . quiet footfalls . . . someone was there.

A voice said: 'I'll put a couple of bandages on your eyes – cool – it'll do them good.' A damp cloth descended on my eyes and two hands adjusted it gently. What angel was this? The clear voice of a girl, with a Swiss accent, rolled r, hard k and all . . .

'Thanks a lot,' I said. Who was she? The cloth was cool and comforting. Passing my hand pensively over my beard, I considered: one of the hut-staff? Definitely not. No sound; but I knew she had sat down somewhere near by.

'Thanks very much – please tell me —'

'Is it really better?'

'Oh – yes – comfortable.'

Silence. What was there about that voice – clear and gentle at the same time? Of course, a man should not be inquisitive; especially when he can't see.

I could not leave it, though. 'Tell me, who are you?'

She laughed. 'They call me Busle* – the Cat,' she said, in that highly appropriate voice.

That put an end to any thought of further rest. Before my mind's eye, far from blinded, there trooped, on delicate feet, a whole menagerie of cats: grey, tabby, red, blue with greenish markings and humped backs, all on velvet paws —

'I need a fresh bandage,' I said.

The hand was long and slender, I discovered; for, as it adjusted the folds, I held it for a moment.

One thing I knew, now – I must get my sight back immediately. And for that, I definitely needed more bandages. Busle had gone out of the room, but she had promised to come back.

It was dark, and I could see blue, metallic peaks, shimmering outlines of glaciers. I had removed my sun-glasses – things were silhouettes and shadows. However, I was able to establish this much. Busle was tall. Slim down below and rounded high up. Her hair had a bluish gleam in it; it was probably brown, or perhaps darkish-blonde. She had des-

* Busle is a pet name, widely used in Switzerland and really means 'kitten'.

scribed it as: 'Busle-colour, my own colour.' Her face presented itself as a rounded disc with dark eyes in it. Tomorrow she had to go.

I asked her to go to the ice-falls with me, though I could only show them to her, now, in the dark; for by daylight I could see nothing.

The séracs glimmered. Her lips were soft. She was full of warmth and imagination. There could only be one Busle like her, even if I could not see the colour of her eyes.

Three years ago, now.

The train arrived during the evening. Why was I so excited? The neon-tubes of the Westbahnhof vibrated shrilly. I hardly recognized her.

'Really you?'

Up and down the city we went. She was nervous, and walked, as I did, at full tilt. She had a saucy nose and a pony-fringe, and unbelievably long legs.

A café: her hand, her voice. Warmth, clarity, imagination.

Yes, it was really Busle.

Here we were in the grey City by the Danube, with its anonymous masses of people – the blue city by the Danube, with its flowering trees, the Prater, the great wheel; with schnitzel overflowing the plate, with the Wienerwald, its gentle outlines overlapping like stage-settings, right out to the Schneeberg. Trees like in a Japanese painting. And the orange-red sickle of the moon, setting now behind the blue-Danube city's sea of lights.

'How old are you?'

We were under the last of gas-lamps, their gently-hissing light a yellowish-green, on our way down to the city. How old was I? 'Twenty-six,' I said, carefully adding two years to my age; I am usually truthful, but we happened to be the same age, and a man is only a man if he has an age-advantage. Anyway, why ask?

We walked the streets till the sun rose. I knew something more, then. Her eyes were grey-blue-grey-brown. That matched her general colouring – grey-blue-brown-green. Busle-colour. She knew three languages. What a good idea of hers, to come to Vienna!

The sculptor, sculpting, remarked: 'Mars is in conjunction! That's three times I've said it, and you haven't heard me. What ails you?' SO . . . Mars . . . ah, yes. 'Excuse me,' I said. 'But surely it will last for quite a while?' And I went.

She had twenty pairs of high-heeled shoes and travelled all over Europe alone . . . she had an unusually keen colour-sense and collected beer-bottle caps . . . she was always full of unexpected ideas . . . oh, she was lovely . . . and at home she had her own library, she said, fluttering her eyelashes learnedly, full of great, fat books . . .

I leaned forward: there were three buttons to her blouse, one of them was open – by Lollo –!

'You aren't paying attention, Kurt. I was telling you about my library,' said she, reproachfully, her face taking on the look of a dyed-in-the-wool State school-marm. I cleared my throat. 'Yes,' I said. 'Lessing was a great man.' That was a big mistake; with a face set in deadly earnest, she promptly gave me a meticulous briefing on Lessing – or was there perhaps a tiny glint of roguishness at the corner of her eyes? I pulled myself together (so was the blouse by now), with great difficulty producing a variety of consenting and disagreeing answers, which laid woefully bare my knowledge of German literature. Why were her eyes so bright? Why did she suddenly smile? Self destructively contrite, I accused myself: 'Kurt, you are a cultural-defective – that has got to be changed.'

'You are a wonderful librarian . . .' I said. And what a fantastic library you are! I thought.

I bought myself a *Signpost to Literature*.

Meanwhile, Busle was gone away.

Situation Report:

1. Season of the year: trees and finances, green (*al verde**).
2. The Book-keeper: misses my daily pull-ups on the door-jamb.
3. The Sculptor: carving a statue of St Antony (though he has seen Busle and knows Wilhelm Busch, who described the terrible 'temptations of that holy man').
4. Wolfi: regards me as if I were a sick horse when, at the 'Vegetarians' Arête', armed with my new learning, I gave him a lecture on Lessing's plays. 'Don't forget the North Face,' he says. 'Don't you let me down over that one!'
5. Me: I regret nothing. The North Face? I shall apply to the Alpine Association for a grant. After all, the North Face is a top-ranking climb.

A letter from Switzerland! It says Busle can come along to the Matterhorn. When I told Wolfi so, on the Peilstein, he groaned.

There was this letter. And another, and another. While the sculptor hewed, I lay on my bed, my face covered with a sheet of business figures, and dreamed – a climber caught between 'ought' and 'has'. Oh,

* i.e. 'the money is finished'.

Busle how you have changed the life of this book-keeper summit-stormer! 'Ought and Has'? One has what one has.

Eyes deep as the blue-green lakes of the glaciers . . . an ice-wall with a pony-fringe . . . but no, the temperature's all wrong . . . Vesuvius . . . Sophia Loren . . . the desert . . . camels with their rocking gait . . . camels with resolute gait? In high-heeled shoes? That was the trouble, she never walks the same way. *Tarab!* – trot! Daisies, nodding, nodding.

The North Face of the Matterhorn, with its nodding gait . . .

The North Face!

My request to the Alpine Association!

I almost choked for want of breath.

Final instalment . . . 'request a grant from the fund for top-ranking climbs'. Well, I had done that.

The North Face of the Matterhorn, with its nodding . . .

Hey! No arguments about its top ranking; it ranked much higher now – wasn't Busle coming along?

Fate moved on rapid feet, now. *Signpost to Literature* in my baggage, off I went to Switzerland.

It all moved so quickly. Helvetia is used to victories. Moorgarten and Sempach: that is where the Austrians were beaten, as every Swiss child knows. Eyelashes flutter knowledgeably, but very sweetly.

There was no doubt about it. She meant it, in good earnest. So, I suppose, did I. None the less a kind of wonder, a sort of amazement fell upon me. I, to marry? That was the question I asked myself, with the instinctive recoil experienced by all sharers of the same fate, down whose back the thought of that unfamiliar legal status has sent coursing a light shudder.

It passed. Remember Moorgarten and Sempach? And now '*Tu, Felix Austria, nube!*' Austria the fortunate, go marry!

I was as radiant as Jove and sent a card to my tame astrologer. As a prudent Austrian, I stipulated a breathing-space – two years. Time to finish my studies.

After that . . . what rapture! What a lovely world! (Only first I shall have to make friends with that dog.)

Permission to make our attempt. Financial aid guaranteed. Our summer of the North Face is guaranteed.

This time we shall get our North Face, you Matterhorn: your top-ranking North Face!

. . . . .

Foaming breakers; cliffs rising sheer from them. When the waves suck back, all the shingle in the bay rustles. Great and eternal is the Ocean.

I wrote to Wolfi: 'Busle and I will explore the conditions on the North Face and, until you come, I shall get acclimatized to altitude.'

The sweet-scented trees were in blossom and the sun shone. Altitude: zero – a good place to start from. On our napkin-holders was written: '*Signor Lui*' and '*Signora Lei*'. We fed on mussels, Asti Spumante, top-grade '*fritto misto*': top-ranking . . .

Silent stood the Matterhorn and said nothing. Sure, Wolfi and I would climb the North Face.

Dandelions and daisies. Our tent stood close to the glacier's edge, at nearly 10,000 feet. Wolfi was still on a training-course with his Section. A wintry-looking Matterhorn peered through the clouds.

'You needn't come for another ten days,' I wrote to Wolfi. 'There's a horrible mass of fresh snow on all the faces.' All I had left was a big bag of polenta. Top-ranking polenta. And the treasury? Down at sea-level.

That night I dreamed for the first time of the Central Administrative Committee of the Alpine Association. There was a green-clothed table and a great many silent faces around it, looking at me, and still looking at me . . . edelweiss, lulled beneath a black storm-cloud. Postponement of sentence.

A green meadow; dandelions and daisies!

'You moaned something awful in the night – is anything wrong?' Busle questioned me, genuinely worried.

'I dreamed of my record of tours – I think we ought to climb something, you know.'

'Oh, yes – how thrilling – let's go straight for a four-thousander!' she cried, her eyes shining.

'The Breithorn.'

We did it by the ordinary route: six hours of solid slogging.

That night I dreamed of the Association again; the expression on the faces round the table had not altered. They looked sad and troubled. One head was being shaken. Wisps of blue cigarette smoke formed the word: 'top-ranking?'

'But I don't smoke; my solicitor can confirm it!' Busle was shaking me by the arm. 'Have you a law-suit running?' she enquired.

Yellow blew the dandelions – exactly the same colour as the polenta. Yellow, yellow and again yellow.

'I can't look at that stuff you're cooking, ever again. I shall die of starvation' . . . and two great tears welled out of those glacier-lakes. I was at my wit's end. 'I'll make you some porridge' . . . 'Well, that would be a change,' she sobbed. Something made me cast a glance forward into the future.

'You know, you'll have to learn how to economize,' I said.

'Oh! . . . xhuatzl ch – Ch – Ch . . .'

Bluish-green flashes of lightning, and a yellow one, as the polenta-spoon flew towards me . . .

'Chaibech – ch – ch . . .' (Please stop it, Busle dear. You are absolutely right. It was *not* the right moment . . . I'll fetch the spoon) . . . ch . . .'

We made our peace.

'I'll go and get a job,' she said, 'down in Zermatt, when Wolfi comes and you start up the face – so we won't have to economize so much.' Oh, you wonderful, wonderful Busle!

But that wasn't enough. Another dream: through yellow polenta a radiant vision of Wolfi in golden corduroys, ringed by a maharajah's aureole. He still had his grant.

He would be arriving in three or four days.

The broad ice-block of the summit, the sheer precipice falling from its skull-cap. There it hung, two thousand feet above our heads, crowning shadows, slabby rock, terrifying grey ice, a whole façade of houses up there, blue, chill, shining in the early light – dangerous . . .

'To think that Welzenbach survived all his ice-climbs,' growled Wolfi. Under a hanging-glacier one isn't safe even at night. Now was the most dangerous time – soon the sun would have warmed the ice up there, playing havoc with the tensions. Suppose one of those street-car trains came thundering down . . .

We panted on up the tortuous couloir of the Breithorn's north-west face, crawling on all fours, ice-hammer in one hand, piton in the other, moving simultaneously, not belaying, Wolfi and I, moving as quickly as we knew how. This broke all our rules, but here the danger of a slip was less than that menacing us overhead.

'Look out!' A shadow flew past us, slicing the air quite close to us. Then silence.

It was our first training-climb for the North Face enterprise. We climbed Willo Welzenbach's great route through the North-west Face of the Breithorn in eight hours. Not bad time, but then, not particularly good, either.

Situation report:
1. Wolfi: 'We aren't in top form – more especially you!'
2. Wolfi again: 'Move the tent up from the beautiful meadow

another thousand feet on to rough slabs,' adding, with a meaning glance at me; 'that's the place for an Alpine tent!'
No dandelions. No daisies. Polenta.
3. Busle: Selling apples and pears in a Zermatt fruit-shop. Such is life.
4. Me: Such is life.
5. The North Face: still full of powder-snow. Our next objective would be the Lyskamm.

'Wolfi, believe me, polenta tastes better and is healthier if you add paprika and onions, also apples and pears. Hasn't anyone told you how important fresh foods are for climbers, according to the latest researches?'
'Yes, but . . .'
'Oh, you needn't worry . . .'
'Listen to me . . .'
'All the same . . .'
'But . . .'
'Nevertheless . . .'
The opposition weakened; silence reigned.
'Agreed, then?' 'Agreed!' 'Wolfi you are a decent climbing-partner. I award you the Golden Edelweiss and bars. I'll hurry down to Zermatt . . .' I know the way . . .
'Goodbye, Busle!' I said, as, my rucksack stuffed with Zermatt apples, I hurried off again, up to the Bétemps Hut, in the shadow of the Lyskamm; there was also a sweet melon for Wolfi, No disappointments for him; here I was, though I am not sure that he was convinced by my theory of condition-training, adapted from that of the marathon-runner to the mountaineer.

The icy upsurge of the Lyskamm. Huge white balconies, their surfaces marvellously sculptured. Above them, corniced ridges, against the blue. A thrilling peak!
The North-east Face of the west summit is 3,000 feet high. We climbed it, arrow-straight, by the most direct line we could find. It was a first-ascent, and only seven and a half hours.
A marvellous climb. Wolfi was radiant and so was I. Now we could really think about our Matterhorn North Face!
It was evening, we were down in Zermatt. Busle had gone on ahead, up to Schwarzsee, underneath the Matterhorn. 'You go up to the hut,' I had told her, 'I'll be following quite soon.' That iron man, Wolfi, on the other hand, was lying in the tent somewhere, breathing mountain-

air. Wolfi – *un des purs* as Samivel has it – one of the 'real' ones: every fibre of body and brain now concentrated on the North Face, speaking of nothing else. Two days from now we would be starting up it . . .

I had told Busle I would be coming soon. So I bought a few small things for the North Face; and then, unexpectedly, ran into some old friends. It got late, and later: no question of 'soon' any more. But it is nice to feel comfortably sure that, whatever happens, one is being waited for.

It was midnight when I knocked at the hut door. The place was shut, every bit of it. 'Busle!' I called, in a half-voice. No answer. 'Busle!' – a little louder this time. There were plenty of windows (but which one?); they were all dark, and the wall of the hut smooth.

Surely she must be awake? How could she be sleeping peacefully while I was standing out here in the cold? A dog trotted across the meadow; I did a few knee-bends. She must be sufficiently worried about me to open the window at least every quarter of an hour, to see whether I had arrived? Well, say, at least every half hour! Really, one shouldn't put one's faith in women . . .

In the moonlight a striped cat was promenading through the grass; it sat down to gaze at me with a kind of scornful nonchalance. 'Busle!' The cat gave a jump. My fury kept me warm for another quarter of an hour; then I set about finding a place to bivouac in. No anorak, no bivouac-bag, nothing. What a pitiful object! Wolfi, of course, always has something along with him.

Cardboard-boxes, lumber, pitch darkness – I had got into the wood-shed. Hard beechwood logs, of course . . . how unkind can Providence be?

I couldn't aspire to any higher storey. The outline of the cat showed up again in the door-frame. 'Gschschsch!' It made another jump. No, really – before I let myself remember the whole long night . . . yet freezing isn't much fun either . . .

What about the boxes?

'Oh, Busle' – I wrap myself in corrugated cardboard – 'how can you bear' – I wedge myself into a big rectangular box – 'my getting frozen feet' – a dust of pudding powder, smelling of strawberries comes out of the box, as I push my feet through its bottom and stick my legs into the next carton – 'instead of staying awake' – I cram a reasonably soft macaroni-box over my head – 'unable to sleep, and only waiting for me to come?'

Hard and horrible are the dictates of fate. But I am beginning to believe it was done on purpose. 'Gschschsch!' Is that brute there again?

87

Hop it – my requirement for cats is fully catered for. I am a climber, in training for the North Face. One of the 'real' ones, at that . . .!

What? Can't even turn round any more? This blasted pudding-box! I've grown four-cornered. What if I force it? That's just about all that was needed. What a smell of strawberries . . .

Life is very hard – hard and four-cornered.

Comes the dawn. Bitterly cold. The surroundings begin to take shape and colour . . . SWISS NOODLE PRODUCTS: UNSURPASSABLE . . . In large letters before my eyes. I try to wriggle my toes. OVOMALTINE, THE NATURAL BRINGER OF STRENGTH . . . I have discovered a kind of rocking motion, inside my cardboard fortress, which provides calories. The morning hours are the chilliest. Ah, a ray of sunlight, falling square across the beech-logs, with little points of light dancing in it. Look at those boxes and logs! You just wait, my Busle, for today's thunderstorm, Austrian pattern!

Half a moment, though. No, I must never give her the pleasure of amusing herself at my expense, about my bivouac! Why, I met friends down in Zermatt, and so I stayed there. So sorry, Sweetie, that you waited for me . . . A much better version than my first idea. Ha! Ha!

I climb out of my boxes and emerge. There is Busle, sitting in the sun outside the door. 'Good morning,' says she, quietly, her eyes shining. My words stuck in my throat. Should it be version One or Two?

'Have you developed a sudden passion for Macaroni?' she asked, amiably. I removed the box from my head. Moorgarten . . .

'Sweetie,' she smiled, 'how you do pong of strawberries!'

Sempach . . .

I took my drubbing as well as I could. (No wonder: for the Swiss army is one of the best in the world; but Helvetia decides which corner of the home shall house the rifle.)

It was midday. I was affectionately occupied with Sunspray and Busle's back (we Austrians are reckoned as helpful, unselfish, always ready to atone for a little slovenliness by attention to detail). Suddenly Wolfi came on the scene, clinking with pitons – actually our 'real' one had the pitons in his rucksack, but I could hear their spiritual clatter, as he found me occupied in such unalpine activities, the day before our face-climb – so excuse the poetic licence.

Said Wolfi, wearing his North Face expression: 'You do know we are starting tomorrow?'

I nodded and went on creaming.

Wolfi threw a first warning look at me, then a second slightly oblique one just brushing Busle's back (she never got a mention in his written accounts). 'I think,' he said, 'we should be getting on up to the Hörnli Hut.'

Busle beamed at him. 'Good luck, Wolfi,' she smiled (not without emphasis) 'my Sweetie will soon be finished, and then he'll come.' Wolfi drew a deep breath and looked up at the North Face. Then he sat down.

And now let him carry on with the story:

'... at our feet lay the little mountain lake in which this proud peak mirrors itself. It was not very late yet, so we stretched out in the sun and enjoyed the beauty of the afternoon.

'The mountain soared majestic above us. Its sharply-defined ridges and flanks fall steeply away on all sides. But the most savage and withdrawn of them all is the North Face. The sun only penetrates that wall, almost 4,500 feet high, for four hours a day. There is not much hard snow on that face; for the most part only treacherous powder-snow covers the smooth rock. Two frightening questions kept on recurring to our minds: would we be above the ice-field before the sun loosened the stones, held fast by the frost? Would there be heavy icing on the rocks?

'Time passed. We shouldered our rucksacks. We met people who took smiling stock of us. Our small climbing-rucksacks were topped by a mountain of clothing and other things carefully tied-on with line; and a miner's helmet shone from Kurt's. [Wolfi was always highly scornful about it, likening it to a useful porcelain article – never would he don such a thing in his lifetime! He was to change his mind later on.] Once again we approached the Hörnli Hut looking like two mountain tramps. Everything good happens in threes. [Wolfi, of course, means that this was our third attempt on the North Face; we had been there twice before, during the previous summer.] All around the Hörnli Hut, close to the foot of the Matterhorn, one can hear every language under the sun. There are people examining the Hörnli Ridge through the telescope, trying to discover today what awaits them up there tomorrow. Tired climbers with happy faces passed us on their way down to the valley. They had had their wish. We did not want to attract any attention and did our best to get our equipment into the sleeping-quarters unnoticed. The guardian of the hut came up to us and asked us straight out whether we intended to try the North Face in the morning. It was late, and I tried to sleep, but I couldn't; I was far too excited. I kept on looking at my watch, hour by hour. Once Kurt said to me: "Oh, do stop being so strung-up!" But he must have been feeling just the same.

'At last it was midnight. A glance out at the wonderful sky, full of stars, encouraged us not to lose a moment. We climbed cautiously up old, eroded avalanche-cones, with the North Face, deep in shadow, looking eerily down on us, like a ghost. From below, our route had looked unmistakable; now, we had to search around for quite a time before we found our bearings. At about 2.30 a.m. we reached the lower edge of the bergschrund. It was still so dark that we could not see for certain where it was easiest to get across. Kurt settled it by going straight for it, up the cliff. We came to the ice-slope. A stone whistled past us like a bullet, then utter silence again; the only sound was the crunch of the frozen snow under the pressure of our crampons, and the occasional sharp ring of one piton striking against another.

'Above us, the first rays of the sun were already falling on the rocks. Rope's length by rope's length we climbed on steepening ice at an even pace. Up here our twelve-point irons got little purchase on the hard ice. And now we were getting the first morning salute from overhead. Small fragments of ice, loosened by the sun, went humming past our heads. [The daisies! It really looked like a shower of flowers; but then, of course, *I* was wearing my miner's helmet.] We had to watch out for them very carefully. We kept on diagonally to the right, towards the great concavity in the middle of the face, which provided our route for the next 1,400 feet. We changed the lead after nearly every rope's length. The next time I wanted to bang in a piton as a belay, it struck rock after only a few centimetres. I tried another spot, but there was simply nothing to be done. I shouted to Kurt to take great care. Presently we came to a steep rock-step below the great bay in the wall. I tied myself to a piton, took off my crampons and climbed a rope's length up steep rock. Kurt kept his crampons on. In this way we contrived that one of us was always ready for difficult rock, the other equipped for ice.

'In due course, the stratification of the rock became very awkward and there was a heavy layer of ice on it, so I had to put my crampons on again. Although we were warmly clad, the cold up here was biting, for not a ray of sun had yet penetrated this huge, slanting, open gully. To our right, the wall went winging sheer into the depths to where the crevasses in the Matterhorn glacier looked like tiny cracks. Above us to the left it loomed up, starkly unclimbable. Against these measurements of terrifying might and size, a human being feels very small and forsaken.

'We pressed on, slowly but steadily, upwards. The climbing became very unpleasant, on a regular, thin sheet of ice, frozen bone-hard, overlaying a mass of loose stones. [Hiebeler commented later that the photographs made it look like winter-conditions.] I looked longingly up at a little rock-spur, up there in the sun, where the Schmid brothers had bivouacked.

'At 11 o'clock, we tied on to two belaying pitons and swallowed a couple of lumps of sugar and a lemon. The way ahead did not look too bad at first. The best of it was that the angle seemed at last to be easing-off a little. But how wrong we were! Ahead lay smooth slabs, without a single hand- or foot-hold, furnished with minute irregularities and heavily iced over. As I none the less started another stroke with my ice-hammer, the slip-ring slipped off the shaft, and the whole hammer out of my frozen mitten. A cold shiver ran down my spine and I held my breath. The hammer was caught by a minute projection and hung there, just below my feet. I climbed down three feet and, to my delight, got a grip on it . . .'

[After that exciting mishap, we reached a traverse in deep powder-snow, which brought us on to that part of the wall which is known as the Roof. We were now well above 13,000 feet.]

'The big snowfield lay ahead of us. Just above us the face looked savagely shattered and rocky. We could already make out the fixed-ropes on the Hörnli Ridge, over there. The terrain became more broken and therefore easier. Towards the top the rock became so good that, in spite of our great exertions, we really enjoyed the climbing. We could hear voices on the Zmutt Ridge . . .

'We climbed a last steep gully of shattered, rough rock, and then over a short snow-slope, straight up to the cross on the summit. It was 7.30 p.m. and the sun was very low. Together on the Matterhorn's summit, we revelled in an unforgettable sunset. An enormous sense of joy enveloped me . . .'

Those minutes enveloped all three of us in it. Busle, who had lost sight of us against the sheer size of the face, now spotted us all the way from Schwarzsee as tiny spotlighted figures on the summit. After seventeen hours on the face, we unroped and in the dying light of an undying day started down towards the Solvay Refuge. All our dreams had been fulfilled – we could hardly believe or grasp it yet – for, three times before, I had been on the Matterhorn in cloud. Today everything was clear. At last we had got our North Face. No bivouac, not a cloud in the sky all day . . . Yes, today, all our dreams had come true.

I did an idiotic thing. Dark though it already was, with the lights of Zermatt quivering down in the valley, there in the darkness of the dark rock-world, I leaned against a black boulder with my camera and pointed it towards the horizon. My hand was shaking, the camera slipped on the rock: over the double-edged silhouette of the Dent Blanche, the colours fuse in a wide band of dark blue, red and yellow.

'Cheerio, Busle!'

The little red train was pulling out of Zermatt and moving away along the valley slope, a small red streak . . . then a dot.

The platform . . . suddenly I was surrounded by nothing but strange faces. I grabbed my ice-hammer and started off for the Theodul Pass, in Wolfi's wake, bound for far-off Mont Blanc.

Nobody else climbed the North Face that year. The slopes below the Matterhorn slowly turned brown. One day the soft, broad, white blanket of the snow unfolded itself on them and on the mountain above them. It was winter once more.

The following summer did not see me in Zermatt. I was living in a tent on the rubble-covered Baltoro Glacier, far away in the Karakorum. Another summer came; I was at the foot of the Eiger's North Wall. Yet another and another summer, as the Earth kept turning . . . I never came back to Zermatt.

There is a meadow, packed with daisies. The sky above it is clear and the air is deep, and transfused with light. The wind caresses the slopes. The daisies lift and droop their little heads. They say 'Yes'.

It is . . . it is . . . it is . . .

I wonder, will any one else ever again discover flowers on the North Face?

The daisies lift and droop their little heads.

They say 'Yes'.

And yet, in a thousand years, no single day passes away.

Himalaya: 'The Gift of the Gods' . . . so said Herbert Tichy, as he and his friends stood on Cho Oyu's summit.

It is in truth, a gift of the Gods to stand so high above the world. I ask myself this: does the intrusion into those ultimate heights change a man? Do the Gods, in return for what they grant, exact something from the best-beloved?

No one knows the answer.

The 'Giant Meringue'

Once in his life – irrespective of age – everyone suddenly does something quite crazy; nor does he normally regret it.

The *direttissima* of the Königswand, the hardest of my first-ascents was a fantastically crazy performance, which still gives me pleasure today, though I would not care to repeat it. But then, I couldn't, for it is no longer possible; the key-pitch has since collapsed into the abyss.

That is not to say one couldn't do the *direttissima*, without the 'meringue', today. It could be easier, but I am not sure. For that summit is a Sphinx; and that enormous cornice of ice, into which they carved a complete defence-position during the First World War, and which fell off the mountain after the second climb, is building up again. Who knows what it will look like tomorrow, or in twenty years' time?

Before the cornice fell, my route was repeated, by none other than Wolfgang Stephan, my regular climbing-partner, who for once was missing on the first occasion. For him, that absence had been too much to stomach . . .

He and two others had an even more disturbing passage than we did. One of them came off, though without hurting himself. The following few sentences from my friend's report of their climb will give some small idea of their venture close to the limits of the possible:

'The "Meringue" loomed like a giant balcony above us . . . the nearer we moved to it, the more impossible it looked. . . we couldn't hide our anxiety from one another . . . in the end, a perfect hedgehog of pitons . . . sheer over the abyss; an amazing sensation to be hanging there from those tiny iron shafts, 12,500 feet up, above nothing . . . getting more and more impossible to communicate with the others, planted below the overhang . . . at last my hand was able to touch the rim of the cornice.'

They had climbed the face and reached the bottom of the barrier,

that is the 'Meringue', at about midday. Not till seven hours later, about
6 p.m., did they set foot on the summit. It had taken all that time to
master the key-pitch. The third man came off while retrieving the
pitons, and found himself hanging in thin air, 2,600 feet above the
Königswand glacier . . .

'There was our companion, swinging far out from the face, remote
from all possible contact with it. So we threw a rope across to him and
tried, without the least success, to haul him up. Then Götz hastily con-
structed a block and tackle hoist.' Thus Wolfgang's report.

I do not know whether anyone attempted it again after that; certainly, no one succeeded. A few parties have climbed the face and
reached the summit by a traverse to one of the ridges on either hand.

And how did we fare? I have an ancient account in front of me. Let
it take us back to those fantastic September days, when that blue pavilion
of ice still thrust far out over the gulf below, when the summit was still
'in one piece', and I myself all of twenty-four years old. I was both a
dreamer and a realist then: bewitched by those white lines of crystal,
ready to take any risk to realize the route my imagination showed me,
up that loveliest of ice-faces in the Alps. At least, that is how I – lured by
a mountain's magic – saw it.

A soft wind caresses the summit of the Königsspitze, soughing among
the rocks, sporting with the powdery snow, now and then whirling it in
glittering banners skywards, then falling again to leave the mountain
quiet in the still air.

It is very quiet up here now. It is autumn, with a hint of winter on
many a day. Very rarely does anyone come up here. It is late in the
afternoon: the wide blue vault of the heavens arches overhead, from the
distant cluster of the Dolomite spires to the white heads of the Bernina.
Far down below, in the Sulden valley, the fires of day are quenched and
a dim twilight reigns. The icy sweep of the Königswand, too, grows
darker, that face plunging away from here to the north-east, overhung
by the blue shimmer of untrodden ice-bulges. Slowly the mountain's
shadow grows out into the east. The gnomon of the sundial. Minutes on
the horizon . . .

The wind starts up again, keen in the stillness, plays about the slender
topmost seam of the cornice, leaving a line of glittering dust, outlining
the huge buttress of ice and snow. The sun's rays slant to the summit.
What was that? From the inner recesses of the mountain comes a soft,
almost inaudible thumping. Again, clearer this time, coming from the
north-east, where the giant roll bulks far out over the face. Then silence
again; till, suddenly, glistening white at the farthest rim, the snow

whirls up, farther over now, quite close to the highest point. Lumps of snow go flying, an ice-axe flashes in the sun . . . a head appears, joy written large on its countenance. Up into the sunlight, and on to the summit!

For two hours there is no rest up here, on top. The air is full of shouts, deep holes are carved out of the snow, ropes run out and taken in; till only the last red gleam of the sun lingers on the summit and the darkness of night comes creeping up those mighty flanks. It is all over: here the three of us sit in the snow, exhausted, dead-tired.

And the *direttissima* up the Königswand is fact, now!

I had discovered the mountain years before, when I was still a boy. We were standing on the summit of the Weisskugel in the Ötztal Alps – I had just acted as guide for a Viennese and two girls from Berlin (the latter we already know; but the man from Vienna was, incidentally, not Willi, the hero of our Venediger story); and we were quite excited because we wouldn't make out what the odd-looking peak, sticking out of the clouds to the south, could be. In the end someone told us: 'It's the Königsspitze.' The name is apt, for the peak is regal, and 12,655 feet high.

My next view was a close-up from the top of the Ortler. I was on my own, having just come across the Stelvio on my grandfather's old boneshaker, making my way home from the Western Alps. There she stood in the morning sun, in all her magic beauty. The light fell slant-wise on the delicately-fluted crystal smoothness of the north face. 'That man Ertl,' I thought to myself, 'had a pretty fair idea of what to tackle!' For it was in the thirties that the Munich 'Mountain Vagabond', Hans Ertl, with Hansl Brehm for partner, had made the first direct ascent of the face. High up on the climb, the huge summit ice-bulge had forced him away on to the left-hand ridge. This ridge had been reached, as long ago as 1881, though lower down, by another victim of the spell cast by that face – for once that overdone word is justified in this context; this was Graf Minnegerode, who achieved the first ascent with the brothers Piggera and Peter Reinstadler, three of the best guides in Sulden. They climbed the left-hand side of the face, a less direct route; but without crampons, without pitons – simply in nailed boots and with an ice-axe clutched in their fists. Fifteen hundred steps they cut. And they were the first to climb it.

Albert and I were standing at the foot of the Königswand in the broad, white cauldron of the upper Königswand glacier. It is difficult of access, for huge crevasses and walls of séracs bar the way from below. That is why we had come by daylight, so as to mark our night-time route in advance, for we wanted to be well on to the face by sunrise.

We were tired, and sat down at the edge of a crevasse. We had been stumbling around on the débris of the moraine for hours in the noonday heat, sweating as we built one cairn after another; perhaps a hundred, particularly important among the rocks at the base of the wall, where the route goes up and down, back and forth, in this confusing approach to the white cauldron and above the sérac-walls. We had finally got in from the side. Now we sat, letting the September sunshine scorch our hides – a treat after the snowfalls of the previous days – and taking a look at the face.

Yes, that Ertl, the mountain-vagabond, a man of Nanga Parbat, explorer of jungles, he knew a thing or two . . .

Then we went into details. A couloir, flanked on either side by rocks, leads up the lower part of the face; above it, a diagonal rib sweeps far up towards the ice-buttresses of the summit region. Hans Ertl had gone up it; we intended to climb straight up from the top of the couloir, following a narrow rib of snow which, mounting in a soft curve and growing even more slender as it mounts, soars right up to the first balcony of blue ice, plumb in the middle of the face.

And then, what?

What a route that would be, straight up to the top over the bulge and the cornice! A dream route, forbidden, impossible . . . fascinating. Could we do it? Boring a way through, like moles? Perhaps there was a secret crack? Or a way right over its outside? A way over that giant roll of frozen snow – straight from the confectioner's – a 'meringue'! And so the name was born.

Hans Ertl, too, had wanted to go straight on up. But he had only four pitons, and then – he fell off, as can, alas, so easily happen. The fall quenched the joy of climbing, blunted the drive to press on; and so they turned aside. 'Glued to the smooth, cold wall of ice,' he reported, 'it took us four hours to master this very difficult pitch, the traverse below the summit-overhang.' They reached the left-hand ridge quite near the summit, but the great bulging obstacles remained unclimbed. Never yet had a man reached the summit straight up the face. The King's crown was still untouched.

Albert was no less enthusiastic about the idea of the *direttissima* than I. He was one of those 'old hands', an experienced ice-man, a blue-eyed giant – one of those who surprised us youngsters by not 'doing' anything for long periods and then suddenly, with no fuss at all, tackling something really difficult, as if it were the most natural thing in the world. How then did I suddenly team up with him? This throws some light on the working of our vagabond nature, which is not always the result of planning ahead. A whole summer's climbing in the Western Alps had gone by, and Wolfgang's time had simply run out; he just had to go home. And so, all at once, there I was, partnerless. Should I go home? Well – no. I spent a couple of days messing about on the Drei Zinnen with a young man from Tyrol – Karl Schönthaler, later to be known as 'Charlie'. Then I was on my own again. Should I go home? Instead, I telegraphed the Edelweissklub in Salzburg: 'Send me someone at least up to Pallavicini Couloir standard.' Albert Morocutti mounted his motor-bike – and now he is sitting next to me, quiet, thoughtful, blinking up at the slopes. He is one hundred per cent committed. Yesterday we put in some training on the ice-fall. Tomorrow we are going to start up the face . . . though we did not know it would be in vain.

Someone knocked. It must be the hut-keeper. 'Thanks!' Two-thirty. One leap out of my bunk and across to the window. Yes, the stars are out. Fine weather.

Then the familiar humming of the Primus-stove, the flicker of the candle, breakfast. The last items go into the pack. That's the lot!

Out we go into the clear night, where not a breath stirs. In the cold out there, our footsteps are the only sound. Abnormally tense, we kept on glancing up at the mountain's dark silhouette. Then the glow of our lamp showed up our first cairn; there it stood on the grass, built of red and blue jam-tins, slightly crooked and helpless-looking, but a masterpiece of our own making. We had to laugh. 'Now for the genuine Chianti flask, which we finished yesterday!' 'Oh, I thought the next one was the tin of donkey in oil?' Over there, something was fluttering, almost ghostly, in the darkness: the economics section of yesterday's paper – in black and white, such a help towards spotting a cairn in the middle of the night! Slowly we lost height, till we met the glacier's level. There, on a particularly lovely cairn, was the Lollobrigida in all her beauty. We began to move upwards again, finding our way easily enough, thanks to the decorated cairns, drawing ever nearer to the mass of dark rocks on the other side. We reached them in about an hour from the hut. It was still pitch-dark.

We stumble upwards in rubble and sand, finally roping up on a small shoulder of rock. In the first pale light of dawn I start up a brittle chimney, feeling my way up, my pocket-lamp in my mouth. Almost at once, out comes a hand-hold. 'Look out!' I yell; but it had already reached the bottom with a crash. Luckily, Albert was safely under cover. and there was no damage to the rope.

Up on the glacier there was already a fair amount of light. The whole face of the Königswand rose bathed in a peculiar greenish-yellow hue. On we went, across the smooth, hard surface; when it steepened, we stopped to put on our crampons. A shout from my companion drew my glance upwards – the sun was coming up. The icy summit ramparts glowed a brilliant red; slowly, softly, the lave flowed down from rib to rib, from hump to hump, leaving only the deep runnels in greenish blue shadow. Even around us, down below, the slopes and séracs caught a faint shimmer, reflected from the shining wall above. Presently the first rays met us, as we were busy adjusting our crampon-straps, and a golden, glittering stream of thousands of tiny crystals shot up towards the sun . . .

A puff of wind came across the glacier. The air was set in motion, gently stroking the slopes – and it was daylight. As we traversed below the Mitscherkopf, the first stones began to fall, counselling us to keep on the move. Threading our way through huge crevasses, we reached the foot of the wall, at the base of the couloir; nothing to be seen above it from where we stood.

At 7 a.m., later than we had hoped, we were at the bergschrund. We stopped to empty a tin of milk, chewed a couple of dried prunes, and got the ironmongery ready. The upper lip overhung a long way, protecting us; but only a little snow came trickling down, not a stone, not a fragment of ice. It was all lovely and quiet? Well, we should see, later on.

I went at the slope above the gash, with an ice piton in my left hand, the ice-hammer in my right; to get over the bergschrund I cut some steps and hand-holds. Then came the first surprise: 'Wash-board snow!' It was fantastic: the surface consisted of innumerable little transverse ripples, hard as bone, some white, some blue, forming a pattern like Grandma's washing-board. Something between snow and ice, sometimes both. What mattered was that this concoction provided a veritable Jacob's ladder to the sky. What incredible luck! Never before in my life . . .

We gained height rapidly, in those ideal conditions. Those blue and white ripples were so fashioned as to afford ample foot- and hand-holds. It was only at stances that we hacked out a step. Albert beamed, and I beamed back at him. There were a few vertical pitches – rock-islands hidden beneath the ice – quite a lumpy world. But what a joy! For several rope's lengths we forgot any question-marks hanging over this marvellous blue September day.

There was a yellow knob of rock above me; to its right, in the sunshine, everything above shone white. The couloir above us was barred by insurmountable pitches; we had to move across, up that way. I worked my way up towards the knob, zig-zagging between sheer ice, snow and passages of rock. The face had become pretty steep hereabouts: I looked diagonally down the couloir below me. I stopped to knock a piton in and snapped a carabiner into it . . . At that moment the 'meringue' came into view – way above us, 1,500 feet or more overhead, a great pavilion, hanging repulsively in thin air, tons of ice balanced out in the blue of the sky, so simple, so motionless – and oh, how it overhung! It seemed quite crazy that it could hold firm, that not a morsel of it came down; but then, it was autumn.

One summer's day it swept two to their death just here, when some of it broke away. I thought of the seconds while they waited helplessly. Today only a few small snow-crystals came dancing down the slope. Today there was magic in the air – and that giant bulge hung up there, as if under some spell.

Are we climbers fatalists? I suppose, in certain situations, we sometimes come fairly near it . . .

Meanwhile, 1,500 feet above our heads, the thing still hung quietly in thin air.

Hours went by. We were in the midst of an extraordinary world of ribs and more ribs and flutings, all going upwards. We chose one and crawled up it, as usual, on all fours; two tiny black dots on that vast face.

Now and then we glanced up at the ice-ramparts above: over the first blue bulge, to the 'meringue' itself. We had got used to it by now, but the nearer we drew to it, the more dauntingly the question hung over us – where was there a way through? A fine powdering of snow and ice came rippling down, but nothing worse; the sun had disappeared behind our mountain and we were in shadow, as we pushed on up towards that first blue bulge. It seemed close enough to grasp, but we never seemed to get noticeably nearer to it. Rope's length after rope's length ran out. Time had lost all meaning. Below us our snow rib lost itself in the gulf, our footsteps up it looking like a column of windows in a skyscraper. Everywhere around us, similar slender ribs swept down into the depths, concentric, like the rays of some gigantic fan, whose top we were trying to reach. Down at the very bottom flashed the mirror of the Königswand glacier's sunlit floor, the overhangs above our heads reflecting its sunny brightness.

At last the snow on our seemingly endless rib grew thinner. Then it petered out into sheer ice. Now down below, I hadn't really bothered my head very much about that first ice-bulge. Just an ice-bulge – so what? Here, the old story was repeating itself: an ice-pitch, at a distance, is just that; close-to, it is something quite different, something that only shows its teeth when your nose is literally jammed against it. And what teeth! This has happened over and over again to every ice-climber who ever lived. A little farther over there, Hans Ertl once had had to fight it out with this self-same bulge . . .

I worked my way up towards the bulge with the utmost caution over a steep slab of black water-ice, of execrable toughness. It took all I knew to cut holds in it. High time, now, to bang a piton in. I tried; but before it even held, there was a sudden crack and an ice-cake a yard long went hurtling down into the depths, almost upsetting my balance. A damned near thing that! At last I managed to get it in with innumerable tiny strokes of the hammer; but on the bulge itself, no matter how I tried, no piton would hold: not the thin flat ones, not the hollow-stemmed ones, not even the extra-short ones . . . Resigned as a burglar might be, finding himself unable to force the glassy security of the König's impregnable keep, I felt my way, with a clatter of ironmongery, back down the smooth slab again. 'No use!' I reported. Our first attack had been repulsed.

It was noon. There we sat on two nicks we had hacked out of the ice, chewing a couple of dry biscuits. What now? Should we take Ertl's route, leftwards, up to the ridge, abandoning the *direttissima*? Or should we have a go, in spite of the wretched ice there, a little to the right, where the bulge broke up into a succession of little pitches, like a blue-tiled roof?

The biscuits tasted horrible. We were only 350 feet from the summit. Three hundred and fifty feet that were the crux of the whole climb . . . Why had the ice to be so bad, just at the crucial point!

Down below, the light was gone from the burnished mirror of the glacier, the shadow of our peak had begun to reach out across the valley. Down there, in the shadowy green, the tiny houses of Sulden shone bright with small points of light. Look, let's get on with it! I got up, slightly stiff from sitting, and started to traverse slowly out to the right . . .

Down in the valley the Sulden guides were astir, and a few end-of-season visitors with them.

'You've lost the litre of red you bet me – they're going up to the right, the Devil they are, as I said; and now it's going to be tough!' Alfred Pinggera bit his lip, jammed his eye to the telescope and nodded. A dyed-in-the-wool mountain guide like him knew just what a hazardous game was starting, up there. And Alfred grinned with pleasure all over his sun-browned face, because he had been sure that those chaps wouldn't turn it in. The other one, who had lost his bet, nodded, too, a little more doubtfully. 'There's something tough doing up there today, all right! The Giant Roll on the König, of all things! Wonder if the pair will do it – the one with the beard, whom you call "The Spirit of the Hills" and that long slab of an Albert, who only blew in here a couple of days ago? It looks barmy to me – those two little dots below the summit.'

As I began my traverse out to the right, I could not guess how many ice-bosses I was going to meet, nor did I know how many litres of 'red' had been wagered . . . It seemed better that way, at any rate, for I was still choking with those dry biscuits.

There, in the shadow, a shining tablet of ice, high above the sunlit world, and steep as a church roof! Never in my life had I hung on such a slab. It affronted my nose, shimmering-blue everywhere, all round me, broken up by almost vertical pitches several feet high.

Taking the greatest care of my equilibrium – not a place to come off, this – I leaned against the wall and hacked out a couple of hand-holds in front of my face: very cautiously, so as not to shatter the brittle ice. A couple more, higher up for my hands. Gripping them, I lifted a foot and climbed gingerly with the front teeth of its crampons into one of the first two nicks, now transformed to a foot-hold, threw my weight on the top two, then on my foot. It held, and so I pushed upwards, straightening myself slowly against the face, and started to gouge out another hand-hold. Over and over again, with the need for the occasional piton; but only Albert's special short ones were any good here, the others simply bent. And so, hold by hold, I wormed my way upwards, nearer and nearer to the great Roll of the 'Meringue' . . .

The tension increased. I hadn't the least idea where we could get through, nor could Albert see a way. All we knew was that those horrid tons of ice hung just above our heads, poised motionless. The excrescence barred the whole face with its stratified layers, an insurmountable obstacle, some eighty feet high, either vertical or overhanging. And so it stretched away, unbroken, to the Sulden ridge, away to the right: only there it was a shade less high.

The main overhang, the pent-house of the 'meringue', was directly to our left, with further balconies behind it, not so easy to see from here. And just behind the great protrusion there was a slight re-entrant. Could it be a shallow groove which would offer a route through those overhangs? Well, it seemed the only faint hope. So: up through the 'meringue' itself . . .'

Easier said than done . . . Hand-holds, belaying pitons, the lot. At last I am directly below the huge wall, with a balcony chest-high in front of me. Very cautiously I push my arms over it to full stretch, and what do I find – a column of ice, with a gap behind it, a real stroke of luck! With cold fingers, I thread a sling through it, snap in a carabiner and, thanks to a pull on the rope and a couple of snake-like wriggles, there I am sitting in a niche above the balcony. The next bit isn't very amusing: head-first, on my stomach, I wallow my snowy way along a closely over-hung ledge. A few more strides, and I am right inside the 'meringue' itself!

All blue. Extraordinary traceries, their curving lines making a grace-ful sweep. I stand, looking up. The vertical has become a meaningless word . . .

The great roof of ice goes winging over my head like some huge dome, jutting out fully twenty feet, then rolling gradually into the depths, drawn downwards by its own weight. I can almost touch the icicles hanging from its lower rim. I stand there, gazing, for minutes on end, overwhelmed by this miraculous blue dome, inside which I am, at the world's most inaccessible place; this dome, a fantastic creation of the winds and of gravity. All the day's targets are forgotten. I am the first to penetrate this shrine.

Albert followed me up, experiencing much the same difficulties as I had. Then off I moved again, tense beyond words as to the possibilities of finding any way ahead. The corner, the 'groove', might be the key; but after a very few steps I could see that our dream of the summit-prize was over. Another balcony, of mushy yellow snow, in which no piton could possibly hold, barred any hope of further progress. The pity of it! Looking up, I could see – hardly fifty feet above me – a narrow seam of gold, the sun lighting the rim of the summit.

We turned back without a word, repeating the crawl along the snow-ledge, the balcony and the traverse to our stance, in silence. Then, foot by foot, as the shadow of the 'König' lengthened over the valleys far below, we worked our way across to the Sulden ridge, looking back again and again.

And then, all of a sudden, I spotted it . . . surely, there, just above the snow-crawl, one small weakness in the ice-armour, and the only one! Three bulging overhangs, but definitely of good ice; higher up, it deteri-orated, but only where it was no longer overhanging. Yes – just at the most improbable spot – there was a way up under the beetling roof of the 'meringue'; then a traverse on a repulsive-looking ledge below the overhangs, a diagonal climb over them to the upper rim of the dome itself, a narrow seam of snow – and the summit could be won!

I knew I should have to try it, however long I might have to hang in the ice; that last link in the *direttissima*. But not today. It had been a day in a thousand. There we stood on the Sulden ridge, looking back, across to the 'meringue', looking down the immense sweep of the Königswand. And there, immune, stood the summit . . .

More snowy days, putting the 'meringue' out of court; at least, in my opinion. Albert and I climbed the North Face of the Ortler. His leave was over, and home he had to go.

And I was alone again. Go home? Impossible. Not without my 'meringue'. Besides, I had the cash for a week more. 'The "meringue", the "meringue", the "meringue"': round and round in my mind. The weather was perfect. The König soared crystal-clear to the sky. Everything was set for the last, decisive effort to make him mine. But I was alone, and the 'meringue' could not be done solo. I simply didn't trust myself. On the other hand, I couldn't leave without it: *suppose someone else were to come and bag it!* I should never forgive myself! It just wasn't on. It was I who had to bag that 'meringue'. Furiously, I washed last summer's socks, trimmed my beard, darned the holes in my pants and sat down beside the path to the hut.

'How about a climb?' I asked the first one to come that way, who looked at all qualified – having first exchanged a few opening gambits about the weather and the surrounding mountains. No joy at all. As soon as I began to unfold my plan in detail, my opposite number lost all interest, or remembered a previous assignment, or had to look after his girl-friend's interests. I started to seethe: 'These damned women in the mountains! How many first-ascents have been scrapped on their account?' It was beyond endurance – though, of course, only an excuse. And this 'meringue' was such an obvious thing!

I went back to Sulden in despair. Alfred was my last hope – the guide. Alfred promptly agreed; indeed, he was enthusiastic. But Alfred's wife, in the next room, had overheard, and invited him to a tête-à-tête. I began to see red – flaming, crimson red.

I am sure Alfred would have come along just the same; but I was not prepared to let my 'meringue' shatter the peace of a whole, long family-happiness. So I passed on – up to the Hintergrat Hut. I knew Fritz Dangl, the guardian up there, a tough nut and a guide, too. Perhaps he would join me?

Up there, a vision of utter peace met my eyes. There on the bench outside the hut sat Fritz, smoking his pipe, with his grandfather beside him. The children and a dog were playing around the place. No wife in sight.

Fritz agreed at once; but he couldn't leave the hut for a few days, till his wife got back. 'Can't you come sooner?' I urged. No, not till then. Abandoning myself to my fate, next day I climbed the North Face of the Little Zebru, so as to keep my hand in. I soon realized that, in spite of my days of enforced idleness – or because of them? – I was at the top of my form. So I opened up a new route to the north-western peak of the main summit and, after a restful little nap up on the south summit, came down by its north face. That turned out to be a rather dicey trip, and I was glad when I got to the bottom. I got back to the hut in the evening, with two solo 'first-ascents' – one up, one down – in the bag. Enough to make one happy. But I hadn't bagged that 'meringue' yet . . .

By now, I knew every inch of it by heart – Fritz has a super-telescope – and I was banging the pitons home where they belonged, in my dreams.

I heard that a couple of youngsters – probably 'Extremists' – with heavy rucksacks, were on their way from Sulden to the hut. I went to look, and came upon a tent. Here they were, two Austrians. We reached agreement in no time. Tomorrow we would meet on the summit and attack the 'meringue', approaching it from the Sulden ridge, by which they intended to reach the top. I informed Fritz Dangl of the latest turn of events. Then I went over to the Schaubach Hut.

Some reader or other may confront me with the proposition that a true first-ascent should be made in one piece, all the way up from the bottom. Ideally, that would, of course, be the most satisfactory way. However, on some first-ascents of extreme difficulty, one dispenses with a repetition of the pitches one has already successfully pioneered oneself, as superfluous; and traverses in again on another day, to start at the point where one left off before. That is how the West Face of the Dru was first mastered, the Gemelli Arête, the North Face of the Eiger in winter conditions. Nor had I any doubts about the practice, having regard to the extreme difficulties of my *direttissima*. Only the last bit was missing, and it was that bit which still had to be done.

The Königswand was bathed in morning sunshine. I had packed all my ice-equipment and was sitting quietly outside the Schaubach Hut, enjoying a rare little moment of idleness. By rights, those two ought to be in sight on the Sulden ridge by now . . .

Not a sign of anyone. Had they been taken ill, or could there be some misunderstanding? Or had they, after all, changed their minds at the last moment – everyone is entitled to. In thoughtful mood, I looked up at our own route on the Königswand, where I knew each separate boulder. Suddenly, I saw two new ones . . . there they were, my young friends . . .

Nobody has ever got up to the summit of the König as quickly as I did then.

When I reached it, my pair were already just under the 'meringue', having made good use of the steps we had left. But something had happened somewhere on the way up – a hammer had broken and was quite useless. Moreover, they had only five pitons. Hans Ertl himself couldn't have got up here with those. At shouting-distance we joined up. I would bring my equipment across to them. One condition: *I* was going to lead on that 'meringue' – *my* 'meringue!'

Down in Sulden, the guides' hearts missed a beat. That tiny black dot up there was slowly pushing its way across the face – up there, under the giant bulge, 2,500 feet above the foot of the wall . . .

That appalling gulf below my feet! I had dithered before taking the first steps out on to the precipice. However, a look across at the 'meringue' drove me on.

Ice in front of my face. Two thousand five hundred feet of emptiness under me. I dare not look down. Utterly alone. Sheer madness, this.

I am stuck; my nerves have let me down. Trembling, I bang a piton in and hang myself on to a line. Deep breaths. My God! Out with the spare rope, and into the piton, hanging on it, and moving on again . . .

The rope has run out. I have got to untie. The rope goes rolling slowly across the sheer face to the piton, with the lazy swing of a pendulum; obedient to the laws of gravity, it hangs straight down the precipice now, over there, like the second-hand of a stopped wrist-watch.

All on my own again. Only my fingers to rely on, and my nerves. Mustn't think. One step, and a compulsory rest. Another. My life depends on the precision with which I make them.

I have got there. Above me, on a narrow ledge, stands Hannes, air-borne, it seems. A fine piece of work, his traverse across, under the over-hangs. At all events he has retrieved the pitons behind him. How could a second follow him now, unless he 'pendulum'd' across? Unnecessary, now, anyway. Much better like this.

I sent a couple of extra-long pitons up the rope to Hannes. No one

could say what his stance might still have to put up with. We both felt a
lot better after that. Very soon I attached myself to the rope again,
belayed this time by Herbert. Here I am, at last, under that immense
roof again. This time, it has simply got to go!

The first thing was to get up to Hannes, and, seeing what this involved, I plumped for the double-rope. Herbert belayed me along the
ledge – thirty feet of traverse with a cold, overhanging swell of ice at
chest-level, pushing the upper part of my body out into the void. With
the aid of a couple of pitons I reached Hannes on his incredibly airy
stance. Now Herbert could let my doubled rope run out, swinging
across to us pendulum-fashion. There it hung loose below us, moving
slowly back and forth. We looked at the overhangs and I fetched a lemon
out of my pocket. 'Have a bit?' I asked. 'Thanks,' came the slightly
grudging answer: for these two had really wanted to complete the climb
on their own, and had, like as not, sat below the 'meringue' for a while,
contemplating it. Anyway, here the three of us were now, and none of
us would get up without help from the others. For better or worse, we
were all in it together – as in some familiar political situations. There
Hannes and I sat sucking our lemon, each his own half, looking up at
where we wanted to be, guessing where the top might be, hidden behind
an ice-bulge. How glad I was to have *étriers* with me; free-climbing on
the outward pull of the rope on this mighty cornice could only lead,
sooner or later, to falling off. It was bitterly cold up here at 12,500, in the
September shadow. With a clatter of pitons, I was off again, and banged
the first one in. Hannes kept on belaying me to perfection, which
cheered me up. No one wanted to become airborne – down that face –
at this point. I kept on hammering away at that piton. The minutes pro-
longed themselves into hours. This was the toughest ice-climb I had yet
met . . .

To me, dependent from the overhang, everything looked crazy! The
sun stood crooked above, hidden from sight. In went the next piton:
now for the *étrier* . . .

As I lifted my foot, I could for a split second glimpse the spare rope,
far down below, on the slanting face of the wall, seen diagonally below
my crampon points, a thin line like a forgotten shoe-lace. I felt for the
étrier with my points – the thin sliver of my wrist-watch's second-hand
circling before my eyes. I got hold of the rope again, found a new footing
in a space above the slant below me. Thin air, ice-waves, everything at
a tilt. Gravity alone told me where the vertical was. Another piton;
another ice-cake went clattering down into the deeps. At a certain point

I realized that I hadn't enough pitons. With the greatest difficulty I retrieved those behind me, only to bang them in again above.

A pull on the doubled rope! Worn out, I rest for a moment against the slope. Then up again over a bulge, a small one this time. What a grind! but I feel good all the same. I have got so far, and now it is only a question of time. There is only one more vertical pitch ahead, then the slope eases back.

Blue flakes of ice. One of them goes shattering down into the gulf. A fine cake, this! I had thought the pastry up here would be solider stuff. But, even if I wanted to, I could no longer go back now. So, now for a short breather.

I take a look under my arm at the slope below, deep in shade. One huge funnel of ribs and runnels, a gigantic blue fan. And there in the middle of it Hannes' face, drawn with the icy cold. Time to move on! In goes another long piton, at an angle, between two flakes. Cautiously, I trust my weight to it, and it holds. In goes an *étrier*, and I am dangling clear, relying entirely on two small flakes, damn it! But it's no better *inside* the bulge; I know because I've tried it. This is the wind's handiwork. So, on with the dance . . .

God, the piton's . . . coming out . . .!

Down! Seconds prolong themselves into an eternity. I gasp for breath, cling madly to the piton below, hanging crookedly, and start to lower myself. More second, long ones. Fighting . . . hanging . . . standing. Standing arched in space, but standing again. That was close to the ultimate limit, that was! Curse those bellying flakes, curse them! I lean my head against the wall. There, dangling from the carabiner, swings the faithless piton.

Now things are getting really difficult. The ice here begins to be rotten. And it is still vertical, too; the last swell of the face, before it eases off. Here I am pushed out farther than ever, trying to lean as little as possible on the pitons and still somehow to keep contact with the wall on hand- or finger-holes. Presently I find I can occasionally force the shaft of my axe in, and, with a circular motion, hollow out a wedge-shaped hole. Into it I plunge my arm up to the elbow, put my whole weight on it, then repeat the movement on the other side. It is terribly exhausting and I am pretty near the end of my tether. Panting, I lay my face against the vertical snow-cliff. Careful, though! I feel as if I might go flying down any moment. No chance of turning round, either, any more. It's either up, or the long, airy flight, now . . .

On again. Six feet more and I am over that flaky belly. At last the slope begins to ease. At last I can't see anything down below me any more. Less agitated, I lean my face against the slope again.

Hannes was shouting up from below: Why wasn't the rope moving any more? Did I know it was perishing cold? All this in a beseeching tone. After all, he had been hanging from his piton for more than two hours, hardly daring to move, alone on that ice-ledge. He must be shivering to death. Of Herbert, not a sound for long ages, now.

I screamed down to him that the worst was over.

Of my dozen pitons, I have only one left. This one is not for the hammering, I use it in order to make progress. I grip it in my fist, this my sole life-insurance. And now for the diagonal move up to the rim of the cornice. Above me there, a snow overhang, with sunlight playing at its edge – the summit.

Tougher again, as I hack out a few holds in the seam of the cornice. I try to beat a way through it; great masses of white, ice-cold, powdery snow crash on to my face. Spitting and gasping for air, I can feel the strength ebbing from my arms. The blade of my axe flashes in the sunlight above me . . . but, hell and damnation, I'm all in . . .

Try farther out to the left, on the very crest of the 'meringue' . . . Pull yourself together; you know your last belay is miles away down below there! I move across, plunging my piton into the snow at every step – my very last piton, my lucky mascot . . .

Now I am on the very crest of the 'meringue'. The summit *must* be close overhead. With great care I batter down the last small rim of snow. Just above me, the wind is whirling glittering snow-dust high into the air. I ram my axe in and haul myself up. One last little bit, one last output of strength and then – I am up on the summit in the full blaze of the sun!

Later, we were all three together up there. We did not hurry away, for our coming descent in the darkness gave us no qualms; we were much too strongly under the influence of the events of the past few hours. We sat in the snow, eating a bit, talking – always coming back to those incredible hours, to the same marvellous thing . . .

The summit is empty now, quiet as it was before we came. True, the snowy surface is disturbed, and there is a deep breach in the narrow outer hem of the cornice. But the wind will come rustling there again, stroking the snow, softly smoothing the hollows, and getting on with his eternal architectural work. And in time he will efface every trace of us.

Tempest

Today the giant banners of the storm are flying from the Lyskamm's summit; the cornices asmoke with blown snow. Pressure-waves go buffeting through the air, there is a rattle of ice-darts, pain numbs your face. The blue, blue sky is filled with the organ-notes of some mighty symphony. This is the soaring tempest of the high places!

One of nature's most stupendous manifestations, it clutches at your very heart. Bent double, you almost float on the waves of air, staggering to keep your balance, covering your face against the stinging volleys of those icy particles . . .

This may all be happening on the Lyskamm — but today's fury is the great storm of the Himalaya: the mighty tempest of the high places, ice-cold, merciless, tremendous, under the wide blue vault of the sky.

See to it that you don't lose your gloves! Take care not to be blown bodily off the ridge into limbo!

Safely back in the valley, the rushing roar of the air is still in your ears and the joy of it remains with you: for that is just how it must be in the far-off Himalaya — as tremendous as it was up there today . . .

My First Eight-thousander

TO BROAD PEAK WITH HERMANN BUHL

Day was drawing to its close over the Baltoro peaks. The shadows of the giants lengthened slowly across the broad floor of the glacier, merging to form a silent sea of darkness, from which the mountains rose like fiery islands. The sun drew down in its quivering, flaming glory towards the horizon. Then – in a magical interplay of lovely colour – only the summits of the eight-thousanders shone high above the world, their snows glowing a deep orange hue, their rocks brownish-red, lit with an unearthly brilliance. Two men were standing on a peak, still breathing heavily from the ascent, their limbs weary – but they did not notice it; for the all-enveloping glory of the sun's low light had encompassed them, too.

Deeper and deeper grew the colours. The last rays of light now rested only on the topmost summit-crests. Then, suddenly, as they looked eastwards beyond the rim of snow at their feet, they saw the wide shadow of the mountain cut a swathe out into space, till it lay as an immense pyramid athwart the Tibetan haze and thrust beyond it, far out into the infinite.

No dream-picture, this. It was real enough, and it happened on the 26,404-foot summit of Broad Peak.

I owe it to Kurt Maix, the writer about mountains, the climber, the man who understood the young and had himself remained young – as anyone who has read his book about the South face of the Dachstein knows – that Hermann Buhl invited me to join his 1958 Karakorum Expedition. Maix was president of the 'Reichensteiners', that small, intimate Viennese section of the Alpine Association, of which I was already a member; and when I came back from doing the 'Giant Meringue' on the Königsspitze, it was he who said: 'You ought to go to the Himalaya, that's where you belong.'

The peaks of the Himalaya – they had always been my dream.

So they had, too, for Hermann Buhl, the man who had climbed Nanga Parbat solo, the man who looked so small and light, not in the least like one's idea of a mountaineer. At first sight, one hardly noticed his tremendous will-power; yet he had set out alone from the last high camp below the Silbersattel to climb the summit of that ice-clad giant, on which attempt after attempt had failed over the years and which had already claimed more than thirty lives. Without oxygen, taking only his rucksack, an ice-axe and ski-sticks, he went up alone into the dark skies of the death-zone, into a world where none can exist for long. Hermann Buhl, the 'loner', got to the summit and came back; badly frostbitten, after unimaginable efforts and perils; after spending a night, at over 26,000 feet, standing erect on a narrow stance; hearing weird voices, tottering with exhaustion, at the very limits of his being. For his safe return to the valley-levels he had to thank, first and foremost, his incredible will-power. So long as a spark of life was left in him, he would never give in.

I only knew him from a distance – I had seen him once or twice at lectures, and heard much about him. He had some of the quality of the great Himalayan peaks – for me there was something unapproachable about him. Once, after a lecture, he wrote 'Berg Heil!' on my Alpine identity-card, and from that day I regarded it as a mascot.

So Kurt Maix introduced me to his friend, Hermann Buhl, and suggested me as a candidate for his expedition, which was due to leave in a few months, in the following March. I shall never forget that moment in the room where Kurt Maix wrote his books, when for the first time I stood face to face with Hermann, fearing the wrong answer to the dream of my life, opposite the slim, light-limbed mountaineer with the lively, dark eyes, the thick mop of hair, the prominent nose – and, in the background, Kurt Maix's cheerful, weatherbeaten face. It all happened so quickly. Buhl talked to me briefly . . . the North Face of the Matterhorn, eh? . . . so you are a student; do you think you could act as an expedition doctor? . . . that 'Giant Meringue' was a bit dicey, wasn't it? I agreed: it hadn't been easy, but magnificent stuff. He gave me a cursory but friendly glance; then he said, 'All right, you must join us.' Cloud-capped ridges, an endless ocean of peaks burst on my eyes – what had happened to the walls of that room . . .?

Maix was already telephoning through to the Press. The Austrian Karakorum Expedition had acquired a fourth member. Name: Kurt Diemberger. All right: D for Dora . . . and berger like Berg – mountain. Yes, in March . . .

Again, no dream, this; it had really happened.

We went by sea, all round Africa, for the Suez canal was shut. To Fritz Wintersteller and myself it made no difference, the ticket was good for either way; we were accompanying the two tons of our Expedition's baggage to Karachi. Fritz came from Salzburg and was a first-class climber, as was Markus Schmuck, the fourth leaf in our four-leaved clover. At twenty-five I was the Benjamin of the party by some years. Fritz, a quiet easy-going type, who rolled his own cigarettes even on the summit of Mont Blanc, was our 'Minister of Food'. The smaller, quick, wiry Markus possessed a first-rate administrative talent – in the end, Hermann had handed the over-all leadership of the expedition to him. He himself remained in charge of all climbing matters, and while actually at work on the mountain; then, even the leader of the expedition became subordinate to him. Hermann and Markus were to follow us by air; in the meantime they were still busy at home whipping up the last money that had not come in yet.

So we sailed on – right round Africa – soaking-in a thousand impressions – the sea, an occasional glimpse of the coast, the colourful life on board, the wide horizons, a visit to the top of Table Mountain. Every day, for a whole month, the ship travelled the length of Austria – it made one realize the immensity of the Dark Continent. Secretly, when there was no special celebration aboard, we toasted Nasser – for having closed the Canal. Then we did another thirty laps of the main-deck, at a trot, so as to keep fit.

Our approach-route lay through the valleys of Kashmir's Baltistan. Each day we and our sixty-eight porters covered a stage of about ten miles, sometimes even less. The tempo was typically Asian; we were destined to get used to it during the next three weeks. The porters normally carried a 60-lb. load, though a few of them humped slightly larger ones. Every mile or so, sometimes even sooner, they took quite a long rest. Then the word 'Shabash!' ran down the long, irregularly dispersed groups of our column of bearded men, and they set down their loads supported by cords running across their shoulders, either on some wayside boulder or on a thigh-high, T-shaped wooden prop – a kind of rudimentary walking-stick – which each of them carried. Or else they sat down, made tea, heated stone slabs and baked chapattis on them – unsalted flat-cakes consisting simply of flour and water – sang and danced to a rhythmic clapping of hands.

We had travelled north from Karachi by train, through the wide, endless plain of Pakistan. From Rawalpindi we continued our journey by air, across the main Himalayan chain. We flew past Nanga Parbat, but saw nothing of that mighty peak, for clouds enveloped it entirely. After a flight of two hours we touched down on a runway of sand at Skardu, capital of Baltistan, a place which boasted 5,000 inhabitants. There we waited some days for the porters to put in an appearance, which they did eventually; we were assured that this represented a fair degree of punctuality. Then we set off northwards, on our way to the great ice-fortresses of the Karakorum, whose distant gleam Hermann had glimpsed from the summit of Nanga Parbat . . .

'Shabash!', the slogan of our 130 mile-long approach-march. However, one acquired the virtue of patience, shedding the vice of Europe's frantic haste. From the Indus we followed the Shigar, and after that the Braldu, through desert-like, arid valleys, barely reached by the monsoon that breaks on the main chain of the Himalaya (actually their water comes down from high and distant glaciers); valleys full of sand- and débris-flats, shimmering in the heat of the noonday sun, while unnamed white peaks floated in the sky like some mirage.

Then, suddenly, we would come on an oasis, rich with early green and pink clouds of apricot trees in blossom – hundreds of them, foreshadowing the ripe fruit we should find on our return journey. It was spring now, early April; we should not be passing this way again till summer.

The broad valley of the Shigar gave way to the savage gorges of the Braldu. The picture of a suspension-bridge consisting of three interwoven plaits of willow-branches still reminds me of the following conversation between a traveller in the Himalaya, well known to me, and the mayor of a local village . . .

'We shall be crossing that bridge tomorrow. Is it safe?'

'Perfectly safe. You need not worry: it will hold.'

'How often do you rebuild it?'

Quoth the mayor, after a short pause: 'There is no need to worry. We always rebuild it just before it gives way.'

A lover of the truth, at all events.

At every place we came to, I found myself fully occupied – in my capacity as 'doctor'.

Doctor? 'Well, you have been a student,' Hermann Buhl had said. 'Someone has got to act as our doctor!'

I had indeed studied – international trade. So I bought a book called '*Vademecum*' (literally, 'come along with me'), took a short course in administering injections, persuaded a doctor to explain the more important diseases, and presently found myself the proud possessor of 60 lbs. of medical supplies, neatly done up in bags labelled: 'Nose, ears, eyes, frostbite, pneumonia', and so on. For dentistry I was equipped with a single pair of all-purpose forceps. I never used it.

Now, my poor confiding patients waited in a queue – the healthy and the sick – while I punctured blisters, squeezed drops into eyes and ears, sounded chests. Fortunately, I had a good supply of pain-killing tablets,

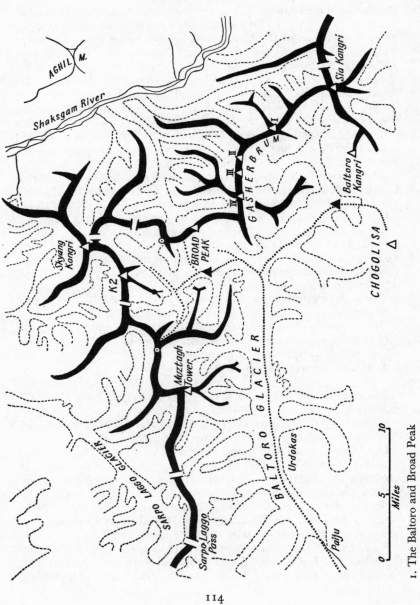

AGHIL M.

Shaksgam River

Sia Kangri

GASHERBRUM

I

II

III

IV

Baltoro Kangri

Skyang Kangri

K2

BROAD PEAK

CHOGOLISA

Baltoro Kangri

Muztagh Tower

BALTORO GLACIER

Urdokas

SARPO LAGGO GLACIER

Sarpo Laggo Pass

Pajju

10

5

Miles

0

1. The Baltoro and Broad Peak

for doubtful cases. You see, unlike at home, nothing could be allowed to go wrong, and I had to exert special care in my therapy – for I knew we had to come out again by this same route.

There were, however, occasions when I really could do some good.

After marching nearly a hundred miles, we arrived at Paiju, the last pathetic clump of trees and flowers. Before us, huge and rubble-covered, lay the tongue of the Baltoro glacier, bordered by its sharp containing peaks.

Alpine Technique on an Eight-thousander

Hermann Buhl was well-disposed towards me. I knew it from frequent small touches, such as suggestions he might throw out, and I was glad. He would sometimes explain to me, in a paternal manner, things I knew perfectly well already; but when I saw what pleasure he took in imparting the knowledge, I refrained (sometimes with difficulty) from saying anything. Certainly, I came to know Hermann in a very different light from that in which many of those with whom he 'crossed swords' picture him. Of course he was a difficult man – that did not escape me, either – an extrovert individualist, thin-skinned, and sensitive as a mimosa – but a man in whom there burned an eternal flame for his mountains. Many who did not possess the same degree of burning vision tried in their own fashion to explain things that were crystal-clear to a Hermann Buhl. He never compromised. His zeal knew no limits – and in pursuing his aims he could be unbelievably tough with himself and with others. Not everybody understands such a man.

I wrote, and dedicated to him, a final chapter for his book '*Achttausend, drüber and drunter*'.

One morning, at Paiju, Hermann issued me a light-hearted invitation to go on a reconnaissance with him, and I gladly agreed . . . We stood on a high shoulder of the savage granite pinnacles of the Uli-Biaho group, looking up at the huge Paiju Peak, across at the rusty-brown cathedrals of the Trango Towers, and up the Baltoro glacier's immeasurable length, farther and ever farther – to where, twenty-five miles away, soaring above the stratifications and bosses of its rubble-covered icestream, the eight-thousanders stood ghostly, unapproachable, incredibly high, not of this world. And there we saw our mountain, our Broad Peak. And two hearts leaped for the joy of such a day.

Now we began talk about our mountain much more frequently. We were all full of enthusiasm and zeal, as was indeed essential, for the undertaking which lay before us would demand the last ungrudging effort each of us could contribute. No one had yet succeeded in climbing an eight-thousander without using high-altitude porters; this is what Hermann wanted to attempt. His plan was that from base camp onwards there would only be climbers on the mountain; they would do everything, load-carrying, establishment of camps and, finally, the assault on the summit. And it was all to be done without the use of oxygen; we were all to achieve high-altitude acclimatization during our load-carrying up to the high camps.

It was certainly a novel concept, tough and not without its risks; but we all looked forward confidently to the day that would see all four of us on our summit. Hermann, the only one of us with previous experience in the Himalaya, thought it could be done, and he must be right. At home the plan had led to the shaking of many a head; but then, Buhl's plans and achievements had always been more daring than anyone else's. No one knew where, for him, lay the limits of the possible; nor had he yet found out for himself. Broad Peak, without high-altitude porters, without oxygen: 'The ascent of an eight-thousander, using the technique of the Western Alps,' he had called it. It was a typical Hermann Buhl plan.

And the route to the summit? It was just as daring as the plan itself: it would simply go straight up the steep ten thousand-foot face of the mountain, over a col at 25,600 feet and thence up a short terminal ridge to the summit-crest. It was a splendid, direct route, which had already been recognized as possible and described in the 'thirties by that famous Himalayan explorer, Prof. G. O. Dyhrenfurth. Buhl had chosen that route up the 'West Spur' not only for its directness, but because it was less dangerous than the route by which Herrligkoffer had attempted the peak some years before, leading as it did for quite a long stretch, known as the 'Gun-barrel', through the tracks of ice-avalanches. To be sure, Herrligkoffer's expedition had had no choice, because the West Spur was as good as impassable for its laden high-altitude porters – a consideration which of course caused us no worries. Farther up, our route, and his ran together for a little way; but above 23,600 feet, ours broke absolutely fresh ground, on which nobody had ever set foot.

As to the high camps, the intention was to equip them relatively lightly and with no view to lengthy occupation, in keeping with the character of the summit assaults, which were to start as rapid thrusts from base camp, as soon as the 'ladder' of camps was complete.

One day followed another. We and our porters moved on and on over the Baltoro's world of humps. We were now more than 13,000 feet up, and the halts multiplied increasingly. It snowed during the nights and the cold was icy. We had already survived one strike on the part of the porters; it was clear that the next one was not far off. The shape of the peaks on either hand was beyond all imagination: the needle-sharpness of Mitre Peak, the fantastic surge of the Mustagh Tower, the huge, shining rhombus of Gasherbrum IV, only just short of the eight-thousand metre line – Gasherbrum, appropriately means 'the gleaming wall' – and, last of all, Chogori, 'the great mountain' – known to the world as K2. I have not calculated it exactly, but I am sure that this gigantic pyramid could contain a dozen Matterhorns. Our Broad Peak, the Breithorn of the Baltoro, with its three summits of 24,935, 26,248 and 26,414 feet, bulked ever more massive ahead of us. Ever colder and more hostile loomed its huge west face; it had been the cold and the storms which had forced Herrligkoffer's expedition, in spite of the presence of such experienced men as Kuno Rainer and Ernst Senn, to abandon the attempt. (Senn had gone flying down over the mirror-smooth 'ice-wall', halfway up the face, for about 700 feet, and would not still be climbing had there not been the soft snow of the 'high plateau' to check his fall at about 21,000 feet.)

At 'Concordia', in fresh snow up to our knees, we met with the expected strike on the part of our porters. All attempts at negotiation proved abortive; this time no pay-rise could shake their decision to go home. Too cold, too much snow, they said.

So there we were sitting on our cases – we four climbers, two mail-runners and Captain Quader Saeed, our liaison officer, left, at this moment, with very little to *liaise*. From now on, we were all porters – shuttling our baggage and finally establishing our base camp, at 16,000 feet. 'Very good training for later on,' remarked Hermann.

Four Men on the Spur

Get yourself fit by carrying loads, and get acclimatized in the process . . . in other words, accustom yourself to the altitude by humping a fully-laden rucksack up the mountain so often, and for such long hours, that eventually it does not grind you into the ground, your headaches disappear and you cease to gasp for every breath. At that point you will be going like a bomb; and incidentally the high-altitude camps will also have been established.

On May 13th, a lovely morning, we set foot on the face of our mountain for the first time and pushed on up the gullies and slopes of the West Spur to about 19,000 feet, where we discovered an airy but otherwise fairly suitable platform in the ridge, just roomy enough to take a tent. It lay about 3,000 feet above base camp, and three days later our camp I was in being. We found the long stint up to it easier each day and the process of acclimatization was noticeable; all the same we high-altitude-porter-sahibs all agreed that the West Spur was a pretty steep assignment, and our relief was obvious each time we dumped our 35-to 50-lb. loads at the platform. At that stage, however, the advantage of climbing on so steep a spur became manifest; for, instead of a slow, laborious descent, we were able to go tearing down to the bottom, some 2,500 feet, in a sitting glissade on the seat of our pants, a method which took only half an hour and saved us much time and expenditure of effort.

By May 9th we had already established camp II at about 20,992 feet, under the icy overhang of the high plateau's giant cornice. Hermann and Fritz pitched the tent, while Markus and I brought up the supplies from base camp. During this operation, Hermann and Fritz made a valuable discovery: in the natural refrigerator of the 1,500-foot high 'ice-wall' above the Plateau they caught the glint of a salami, a bottle of egg-liquor and a tin of bacon belonging to the Italian K2 expedition; the last item having been fetched by Herrligkoffer's team from the Italians' base camp. Surely it was by an unexampled circular-tour that the bacon found its way into our cook-pot; the liquid was still excellent and even the three-year-old salami had been perfectly preserved up there, as we confirmed after our first hesitation. At our 'ice-palace' (camp II), below the cornice, we later on replaced a tent which had been crushed by snow-pressure by one belonging to the earlier expedition, found by us on the ice-wall; and we built their fixed ropes into our veritable handrail between high-camps II and III, on that very cliff.

We were still short of one camp, the assault camp from which our attempt on the summit would be launched, a camp III at about 23,000 feet: the last rung in the ladder of camps we were in this way pushing up the face. Unfortunately, on May 21st, the weather broke, with devastating days of blizzards and gales. We sat in our base camp and waited; but on the 26th we were all four on our way up the Spur again in beautiful weather. Although camp III had not yet been established, we had decided to go for the summit. After Hermann and I had prepared the slope of polished ice above the Plateau so that loads could be brought up it, while Markus and Fritz looked after the supplies, we finally joined up and established our assault-camp, at just under 23,000 feet, on the evening of the 28th. Fearing that the weather might turn bad again soon, we dispensed with a rest-day and started out at first light the next morning.

We made good progress at first, but higher up we were greatly

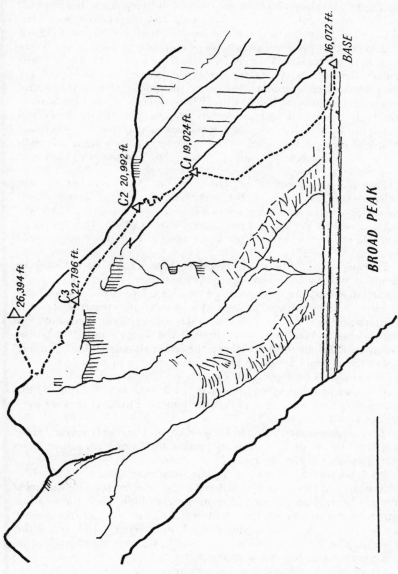

2. The Route on Broad Peak

troubled by the deep-powder snow lying on the steep face and, above all, by the fearsome cold. When the sun's rays at last reached us, we all felt as if we had undergone some kind of a redemption; but this was followed by an ever-growing, leaden sense of lassitude as we gained height. Were we suffering from lack of oxygen? Or was it the effect of the cold we had suffered earlier? Whatever the cause, we moved more slowly all the time. During the afternoon we reached the saddle between the central and main summits, 25,600 feet up! Before us lay a steep ridge of snow and rock. We felt it could not be very far now; perhaps we should still pull it off. By now, however, each step demanded four or five breaths. A couple of rock-pitches called for our last reserves of strength; only will-power forced our weary bodies up, foot by foot, and time was passing at an unbelievable speed.

Fritz was just ahead of me, Hermann and Markus about 150 feet behind us. At last! There, in the level rays of the late sun, above a steep snow-slope, we could see dark rocks clean-cut against the sky. There was nothing higher. We made a last effort. Fritz and I stood on the rocks, with clouds drifting around us. There was really nothing more above us . . .

In front of us, to the south, Broad Peak's summit-crest fell away in gentle curves, swung away widely beyond them – and then – yes – started to rise again! Went on rising, up and up, to form a shining cone of snow, way over there, probably an hour away – the true summit! Perhaps fifty or sixty feet higher than our vantage-point, no more than that . . . but an hour away, over there. It was 6 p.m. – much too late to go on now. Bright mists enveloped the ridge, darkness came climbing out of the abysmal depths. If anyone went on over there now, the odds were against his ever getting back . . .

Down we plodded, 3,000 feet down, back to our assault-camp. By the time we reached it we were all in, utterly spent. Two days later we were all down at base again.

There we were, repeating to each other, over and over again: 'Sixty miserable feet short . . . only sixty vertical feet in height . . . but those sixty feet were at the other end of the mountain!'

Well, we would just have to capture them next time.

Markus and Hermann had suffered a degree of frostbite in their toes. We ate heartily and recovered from our exertions. Then the weather turned marvellous again, clear and beautiful, but icy-cold. We dashed up the spur again, leapfrogging camp I and sleeping at II, below the plateau. The following afternoon, June 8th, we were up at our assault camp once more, just below 23,000 feet.

'Tomorrow, and tomorrow and tomorrow . . .'

To the Summit

It was unusually light in the tent; the moon was up outside. I kept on thinking about the morning and couldn't sleep much. Hermann kept on turning over next to me. The hours simply crawled. We dozed off for a while . . .

Hermann woke up at 2.30. So did life in the tents. Just getting up was a job, for there isn't much room. Nor was there much time for breakfast. Thermos containers changed hands from tent to tent. Then at last we were off!

It was unbelievably cold. Our fingers stuck to our crampons. Ice-fragments went clattering down the slope outside the tent. The thermometer at the tent-door read $-25°$ C. So it must be $-30°$ outside. But it was a fine morning.

We went up over ice and wind-packed snow in the half-light. Not a breath of wind was stirring. Every now and then our crampons grated on the hard ice. Soon it grew lighter; the first gleam lit the high summit of K2. As if by magic, a little later, hundreds of peaks all around us had caught the new day.

High overhead, the Broad Peak summits stood dark, seamed here and there with bright patches. We looked longingly up, to where there was light and there must be warmth, too. The whole of our western slope lay in deep shadow, and the cold increased every minute.

Down there the tents grew smaller at every step, as we moved into deeper powder-snow alternating with wind-caked hard surface. The cold was pitiless, penetrating everything – our huge Himalayan boots, our fur socks, paper linings, everything. Nothing could stop our toes from losing all feeling. The only thing to do was to halt every 200 feet, and swing our legs for a couple of minutes as hard as we could – an exhausting exercise at that altitude. For all our early progress we were now moving forward very slowly. Hermann, who lost two toes on Nanga Parbat, soon had no sensation at all in his right foot. I wasn't quite so badly affected, yet we had been climbing for four hours in this murderous cold. It was 8 o'clock before the first rays of the sun came to us over the col. High time, too; especially for Hermann, though by now I couldn't feel my toes at all, either. The only thing now was to get out of our boots and resort to massage. Presently Markus and Fritz, who had taken a line rather to the left for the last part, joined us and we were all sitting in the morning sun at 25,000 feet. Hermann and I went on rubbing our feet, but it took a long time to get any feeling back into them. Markus and Fritz were the first to get sensation restored, so they took over the lead from us. Eventually we put our boots on and started up after them. My own feet were perfectly all right again and I felt in good form. Not so Hermann's – he had fierce pains in his right one and went more slowly every minute. His old Nanga Parbat injuries were throbbing unbearably in his veins.

The last 700 feet up the final slope to the col is steep, bare ice; the end bit, consisting of some rocks, is very hard work indeed. We got to the col at 1.30, half an hour behind the others. Hermann was in such a bad state that he had to lie down. He didn't think he could get to the top in his condition. I suggested a rest and some food, which might help; but he only took a handful of dried prunes, some glucose and a drop of tea. His foot was hurting him fearfully.

I stared out far into the west. There in the distance rose that solitary giant, which we had already seen from the plateau, the peak where Hermann had been frostbitten, during his bivouac at 26,000 feet. But he had been to the summit first: all by himself, to that 26,620-foot summit of Nanga Parbat. He had paid a great price . . .

There was hardly a breath of air moving over the col, nor a tiny cloud anywhere in the sky. The sun struck down with full force. We had been there an hour, and Hermann felt a little better.

So off we went again.

We hadn't much time left, but it ought to be enough, if we didn't have to stop too often. Our only chance of getting to the top was a steady, unbroken pace. At all events, there was no doubt that our other pair would get there; for, a little earlier, we had seen the tiny figures of Markus and Fritz disappearing high up on the ridge into the almost black blueness of the sky.

Very slowly we moved on up the steep rock- and snow-ridge leading to the subsidiary summit. The ridge was plastered with huge mushroom-like cornices. The horrific precipices plunging from the east side of the central and main summits were clothed in similar amazing snow-structures – mushrooms, ribs, enormous pilasters of snow. The great wall along whose top we were moving dives fully 10,000 feet into the abyss. It almost made one giddy to look down on unnamed peaks 20,000 feet high and the broad rivers of glaciers flowing away to the far horizon. We had the sensation of being incredibly high in the earth's surface. But it was still a long way to the summit . . .

We stopped again to rest. We went on again, fighting for oxygen for our lungs. A few yards farther on, we stopped again. Then, on again. The intervals between rests grew shorter and shorter. Our neighbour, the Central Summit, roughly 26,250 feet high, showed us how slowly we were gaining height, for it was still well above us. At last we reached the rocky step in the ridge. The chimney by which it is climbed demands an output of effort. Hermann braced himself and got up it, but after that we hardly moved forward at all. And we had still not got up to the 26,000-foot level.

We stopped on a little shoulder of snow. It was a quarter to five. Two more hours before the sun goes down. And we had been more than two hours over the short bit from the col up here. The summit was still a long way away. If we ever got to it, it would be in the dark. And then what?

We admitted then that it was too late, and it was a sad and bitter realization. The fact was that it would be lunacy to go on, at our pace.

Could I do it alone? I wondered. I asked Hermann's permission to have a go. He knew how set I was on it, and said yes. I thanked him, promising he wouldn't have to wait very long. I would be back as soon as possible and then we could go down together.

I wanted to say something to cheer him up, but knew there was nothing to be said. There he sat in silence on the snow, staring out into the distance, staring at Nanga Parbat – and, as he sat staring at his own mountain, I knew what he was thinking . . .

If I was to get to the top, I must move quickly; there might just be time. I felt pretty good, as I started off up the ridge again, alone.

That slope up to the subsidiary summit is steep. I was soon gasping for breath. But presently I was above the Central Summit. I gritted my teeth, climbing much too quickly; but I couldn't afford to go slower. I stopped, leaning on my sticks, panting. For a moment everything went round and round. Then I saw Hermann sitting down there, still gazing out into nothingness. Never mind, I thought, I'll soon be back with you again. But now, there's the top up there, and I must get on with it. I wonder how far it is – maybe an hour? I wonder where Fritz and Markus have got to? Perhaps I shall be meeting them soon, now . . .

There they were, two dots on the snow of the summit slope. That's them, and they're still going up. It was a little after 5 o'clock. Come on, I said, don't hang about, there's no time to spare, and Hermann's waiting for you down there. I went at the first great humps like a madman. Then the ridge flattened out, giving way to a mixture of rock and snow. I moved as quickly as I could, shoving myself forwards with my ski-sticks, my eyes fixed on the next two yards ahead. No time now for looking to right or to left. Now at last the summit was coming down to me at a fair pace. My breath was coming in great gusts. I was puffing like an engine. I knew I mustn't stop, or everything would go swimming around me, like a little while ago. Then I was at the last little rise to the summit. My knees wanted to sag. On you go! Only a few yards more. Steep now.

My heart thumping like mad. But there are the last few rocks, the summit snow slope, just over there . . . and Markus and Fritz . . .

They had just finished taking their summit photographs and were on the point of starting down. A minute later I was alone. I stood there, utterly exhausted, and looked back to the subsidiary summit. I had only taken half an hour to come up from it, so I felt I had earned a short rest. I moved up the few yards to the last steps in the trail, at the edge of the mighty summit-cornice, and dropped my rucksack on the snow. What a relief to be sitting down again! My breathing soon settled down to normal and in a very short time the atmosphere didn't even seem thin any more.

Wherever I looked, a sea of peaks met my eye. Far away, over there, the Pamirs; farther to the left, all by itself, Nanga Parbat, 125 miles away as the crow flies. K2 bulked enormous, just above the subsidiary summit – 28,250 feet of it. I looked up at it in awe, realizing that my 26,400-ft. perch was so noticeably lower. To balance that, I looked down and far, far below me recognized a fairly hefty dwarf; it was, in fact, the proud sharp head of Mitre Peak, 20,000 feet high. Beyond, soared Masherbrum, which had lost nothing of its magnificence. Close at the feet of Mitre Peak lay 'Concordia', my eye plunging almost 12,000 feet down upon it. Then I began to look for our route up the long waves of the Baltoro. That browny-green spot at its far end must be Paiju, the last little oasis before we took to the ice. I couldn't take my eyes off it; I hadn't seen a living green thing for six weeks . . . Why, today must be Whit Sunday! At home, now, the trees must be in blossom, the meadows green with lush spring grass; at home, they will be thinking of us. All about me the great peaks stood in an immense silence. I suddenly felt terribly lonely . . .

I got up. From behind the cornice those two magnificent eight-thousanders, Gasherbrum II and Hidden Peak, lifted their heads. Then I looked out to the left of the cornice, eastwards, where the ranges were lower: brown ridges with snow on them, giving way to greyish-brown plateaux, stretching away into the distance – Tibet? That cornice in front of me annoyed me. If one could look out over it without hindrance, it would feel just like looking down out of the sky; a unique sensation, to be up above everything, with nothing but air and empty, infinite space round and about. I wondered whether it would be safe? When I tested it, I found the cornice was solid névé, a nice permanent structure. Finally I stood clear, with nothing between me and the view, nothing but thin air all round me. I gazed eastwards for a long time over those extraordinary depths, far into the unknown, which must be Tibet. An unbounded loneliness lay on that landscape. There was something incomprehensible about it, though what, I could not say. Then I brought my eyes down to the glittering rim of snow at my feet, which was the ultimate edge of Broad Peak. I let my ski-stick roam over the curve of it, but that was the limit of my climbing.

It was time to go. Hermann would be waiting down there. I was on my way down the summit snow-slope, when I stopped in my tracks and took another look around. What more could I want? I had seen everything. I had been on the summit. What was I waiting for? I didn't even know myself.

I hurried on down, leaving the topmost rocks and the summit snows farther and farther behind. At my feet lay the undulations of the long, almost level crest. It was all over. Was I really happy? Was that the hour of which I had dreamed ever since I first set foot on a mountain? Down there on the ridge, my rope-mate was sitting, the man with whom I had hoped to climb the summit. And what about the summit itself? It had been impressive, the prospect from it overpowering; but the picture in my imagination, my fantasy-summit, outshone it by far.

I stopped again and looked back towards the top, with the trail clearly etched in the snow. Yes, it was all over. I had been up there. It was the climax of a climbing-life – it was the Thing itself. But how utterly different. What a pity! My dream-picture was fading into paleness. It is so still and silent up here, and I am tired and very lonely . . .

I hurried down as fast as I could go; but I was no longer moving as quickly as I should have liked. All the same, half of the crest was behind me now; in a moment the subsidiary summit must pop up behind a rib of rock. Hermann wouldn't have too long to wait now. We should be able to get well below the precipice under the col before daylight failed for he would be rested now . . .

Hermann had remained sitting on the shoulder for a while, then he had felt better; so he took an expert's survey of the steep slope to the subsidiary summit. It didn't look so bad, after all. Yes, he must get up as far as that, at all costs. And after that? Suddenly he knew he would go on beyond it too. Slowly, with all that incredible strength of his will, he started to move, very slowly, upwards. The slope was inhuman and never seemed to end. But Hermann's will-power was even more endlessly inconquerable. Yard by yard he drew nearer to the subsidiary summit, and there on its crest he met his two team-mates, Fritz and Markus, coming down. 'How much farther?' 'Oh, a good hour.' And so, trusting to his Nanga Parbat luck, Hermann went on. He was determined to get to the top now, even if it was in the dark.

The Summit of Dreams

I was still up at 26,000 feet, breathing several times to each step I took. It was slightly uphill again. There were the now familiar rocks. Then the subsidiary summit came into view again, with K2 bulking high above it. I took note of it vaguely and looked down over the hump in the ridge ahead of me. What on earth was that? I stood rooted to the spot. A yellow dot? It must be a hallucination. But it was moving, and it was an anorak. It was Hermann. 'Hermann!' I shouted.

How on earth had he managed it? In the state he was in? Nobody else could have done it. I was amazed, no almost shattered, by such an incredible exhibition of will-power. And now, surely, we would be able to go up to the summit together . . .

Hermann kept on coming up, slowly, step by step, his face drawn, his eyes set straight ahead. Then he was with me. I wanted to say what I felt, but the words wouldn't come. I was just glad that he was here, with me.

It was close on half past six. The sun's light lay quite flat on the crest of the ridge. The Baltoro lay swamped in shadow. The peaks below us seemed incredibly plastic in the horizontal illumination. The sun would be down any minute now.

Surely it would be madness to go on to the summit now? I started worrying about it. Our assault camp was 3,600 feet down there; and here we were climbing up into the night. But Hermann Buhl was going on ahead of me. Hermann, who had already once spent a night at 26,000 feet. Why not this one, too? True enough, he had had unbeliev-able luck that time. Would we have the same good fortune now? And if we didn't – what matter? I spent a moment savouring the thought; then an extraordinary thing happened.

Suddenly everything was so natural that I could laugh about it all; about the fears of all the others down below there, their fears about their lives, my own fear of a little moment ago. Now, for the first time, I was truly at one with the heights up here. The world down there lay bottomlessly far below, and utterly devoid of meaning. I no longer be-longed to it. Even my first climb to the summit was already remote beyond words. What had it brought me? Boundless astonishment that it had all been so different from my anticipation, utter disappointment. That was all, and it was all forgotten already. But now the true summit was up there, bathed in unearthly light, as in a dream.

The shapes of the huge snow-mushrooms grew ever more ghostly, their shadows strangely like faces. Everything seemed alive; and there in front of me on the level snow went Hermann's long shadow, bending, straightening, even jumping. It was deathly still. The sun was almost down. Could anything in life be so beautiful?

I stopped for a moment, leaning heavily on my sticks, then moved on, smiling to myself. There was Hermann going on ahead. We were going on to the top together. Yes, we were going to it in the dark; but ahead of us gleamed a radiance, enfolding every wish life could conjure, enfolding life itself.

Now was the moment of ineffable truth – the silence of space around us, ourselves silent. This was utter fulfilment. The sun bent trembling to the horizon. Down there was the night, and under it the world. Only up here, and for us, was there light. Close over yonder the Gasherbrum summits glittered in all their magic; a little farther away, Chogolisa's heavenly roof-tree. Straight ahead, against the last light, K2 reared its dark and massive head. Soft as velvet, all colours merging into a single dark gleam. The snow was suffused with a deep orange tint, while the sky was a remarkable azure. As I looked out, an enormous pyramid of darkness projected itself over the limitless wastes of Tibet, to lose itself in the haze of impalpable distance – the shadow of Broad Peak.

There we stood, speechless, and shook hands in silence. Down on the horizon a narrow strip of sunlight flickered – a beam of light reached out above and across the darkness towards us, just caressing the last few feet of our summit. We looked down at the snow underfoot, and to our amazement it seemed to be aglow.

Then the light went out.

The west face of Broad Peak lay drenched in the pale illumination of the moon. There were deep shadows among the rocky steps of the subsidiary summit. Presently we were among them, looking for the way down. It was not easy and we roped up for safety. The chimney was particularly difficult in the darkness, but just before the col we were out in the full light of the moon. Then we started down the steep face.

Camp was still nearly 3,000 feet below. Hermann felt a little better now, but we were both dog-tired; too tired to risk a bivouac. So, on we went, down and down.

We must have been going for untold aeons. We halted at the edge of a crevasse, nodding. The ascent was a dark memory now. There was still half the descent to be negotiated. Down in the depths there was a vague gleam, which must be the plateau. It gave us the rough direction, but it never seemed to come any nearer. It seemed quite impossible to get any nearer to it.

'What are we sitting here for? We ought to go on down. It would be lovely to go to sleep.' Somehow we staggered to our feet and started down again. Down and down. Endlessly, eternally down . . .

It was half past one before we got to the tents. We opened the flap and crawled in. In, and into the blessed haven of our sleeping-bags. 'Oh, sleep it is a gentle thing . . .'

Safely back at base camp together, we were all looking up at our mountain, as the evening sun turned its high summit to molten gold. And I gave thanks to fortune for the fulfilment of the greatest wish in my life.

The shining radiance of that great peak will be with me all my days.

Chogolisa

It was by now mid-June. There was a fly sitting on the tent-roof and a spider mountaineering on a boulder. The ice had melted steadily and our base-camp tents were perched on lofty plinths. We were slowly recovering from our exertions and spent the time writing reports and letters: 'All four members of the expedition reached the summit of Broad Peak on June 9th by the shortest and best route, employing neither high-altitude porters nor oxygen equipment . . .' The sun was beating down on the roof of our tent. We were surrounded by the white glitter of high peaks. 'We intend to stay here a little longer and do a few gentle climbs – maybe one or other of the six- or seven-thousanders . . .'

Down there in the valleys it must be high summer. It even makes itself felt a little up here. I lay in my sun-warmed tent and, while the melting ice-streams gurgled away outside, I kept on picking out from among my home mail (we were so much at world's end that the latest the mail-runners had brought up the glacier were six weeks' old) a picture post-card, with a meadow, a tree and, in the background, a little lake on it. On the back was written: 'I am here on a little walking-tour. Tchau!' The card was from Busle, and the tree was a real tree. (How long since I saw a real tree?) Then I re-read her last letter, which came from Norway. 'I have come to the far north,' she wrote, 'I can't describe to you how big that world is – something that I can't explain.' She could not describe that great world of the north, which I had never seen. An odd idea occurred to me. Hadn't I, too, penetrated a great world which I could not describe to anyone, not even to her? Up there on the summit-ridge of an eight-thousander? When I got home would I be the same person I was before I came out here? I took another thoughtful look at that tree. Oh, I should like to be going home this very minute! I looked up and saw the great peaks that ringed us, Chogolisa's heavenly roof-tree, the séracs of the Baltoro glacier. Here I was, once in a lifetime. I wrote her a letter from one remote world to another.

Chogolisa is a magic mountain.

It is so lovely that the statistic of its height, 25,110 feet, seems irrelevant. The British had long ago christened it 'Bride Peak', because it is always entirely clad in white. A white rhombus, an icy roof, high up in the heavens. Dyhrenfurth, when he wrote his book about the Baltoro, remarked: 'Its classic beauty of form and the repose of its outlines stamp it as the ideal ice-mountain.' Only when seen from a distance of some twenty miles does it reveal, at the left-hand end of its great pitched-roof, a minute dark tooth, the small rock-turret of its summit. The mighty south-east ridge, sweeping up for something like three miles, catches the full sun from early morning onwards – a great advantage – and it was as long ago as 1909 that the Duke of the Abruzzi's expedition attempted to reach the summit by it. At 24,600 feet, only 500 below the top of that immense roof, they were forced by a storm to retreat; and, for a long, long time that remained the greatest height achieved by man. Nor had anyone reached the summit since.

On our ascent of Broad Peak we had all marvelled at that beautiful mountain to the south of us; but much nearer, to the west, there had been splendid peaks in the Savoia group which had caught our eye as possible secondary objectives. In the end Hermann, who like the rest of us had made a good recovery while resting at base camp, was especially attracted by Mitre Peak and the Trango Tower; besides which we also wanted to visit the Gasherbrum glacier and reconnoitre Gasherbrum IV – or at least take a close look at it from there.

However, the first consideration was to evacuate the Broad Peak camps. Markus and Fritz, taking Captain Quader with them, cleared camp I; and while Hermann and I went all the way up again to deal with II and III, Markus and Fritz, on short skis, went over to the Savoia glacier and climbed the group's highest peak, a fine summit over 23,000 feet high. This lightning foray came as a great surprise to Hermann and myself, who had no idea they had such a venture in mind. We turned our eyes southwards: we would make Chogolisa and the Gasherbrum glacier our programme. And we, too, would carry it out as a two-man expedition.

The One-Runged Ladder

Chogolisa would demand several high camps, that was obvious. Yet we could not carry more than one tent. The solution was daring: a single transportable high camp – a ladder of camps consisting of a single tent. Herbert Tichy and his Sherpa had worked their way up Gurla Mand-hata in Tibet that way. So our single tent should serve as our base camp and all succeeding camps, I, II and III, as necessary; a single rung in a ladder which we would push up the mountain day by day.

After Hermann and I had decided, during the course of June 20th, exactly what we should need for our attempt on the peak, I went on ahead that evening towards Concordia, carrying about 80 lbs. Hermann who still had some things to fetch from the foot of Broad Peak, followed me early next morning, humping a similar load. Thanks to the marker-pennants I had planted, there was no difficulty about rejoining one another, and we were able to push on together, late in the afternoon, over the endless humps of the Baltoro's central moraine. By evening we had found a marvellous site for our base camp close to the enormous ice-falls at the bottom of Chogolisa, and there we pitched our tent. High overhead soared the mountain's fantastic roof; wherever we looked, we saw nothing but ice and snow.

In spite of that, Hermann thought our climb would only take a few days; after it, we might still turn our attentions to Mitre Peak. The Gasherbrum glacier and more especially Gasherbrum IV were perhaps rather too far to contemplate.

On the 22nd we were already halfway up Chogolisa's ice-falls and laid a depot down on a ridge of hard snow we found there. The next day, the weather was bad; we decided not to wait too long, but to push on as far as we could get.

'June 24th: 4.30 a.m. off with tent; snowing gently; weather nothing special; going very well; 7.30 a.m. depot at 18,000 feet; rucksack, with depot material, about 55 lbs; on up the Spur in knee-deep snow; trail broken all the way to the Kaberi Saddle; about 5 p.m., pitched camp at 20,900 feet; whole route marked with pennants.'

What was the story behind these cryptic entries of Hermann's? First of all, that he was in splendid condition. In spite of the deep snow, he broke the trail all the way up to the Kaberi Saddle and would not hear of my relieving him in the lead. Secondly, that on that first day of ours we climbed 4,600 feet. (These facts should, I hope, convince anyone who imagines that it was an enfeebled Hermann Buhl who tackled Chogolisa, beyond any doubt, that the contrary was the case. Certainly every mountaineer will recognize it.) Moreover we were carrying anything up to 65 lbs on our backs and, in view of our rapid progress in spite of poor weather, our spirits were very high. After heating a drink on our hissing cooker with great difficulty, we went happily to sleep in our first Chogolisa camp.

Next day, Tuesday the 25th, the weather was bad again. We stayed in our sleeping-bags till 10 o'clock, cooked a meal and, at 1 p.m. struck our tent and, in spite of knee-deep snow, climbed to the shoulder in Chogolisa's South-east Ridge, at a height of 22,000 feet. There we erected our tent again, this time as camp II. We were now high enough to warrant a direct attempt on the summit. All we had to do was to wait for fine weather . . .

Towards dawn on the 26th a furious storm blew up. It leaned against the outside of the tent and we against its inside. Luckily we had anchored it well. A few feet higher up, bedlam had broken loose. The wind was screaming over the shoulder with unremitting fury. When at last, after several hours, the walls of the tent stopped flapping, we went out, intending to go up a little way towards the crest we called 'Ridge Peak' and stretch our legs. It was only then that we realized how sheltered our tent-site was. Up on the shoulder we were almost blown away. The rope curved out in a wide festoon, parallel with the ground, weightless, air-borne. Ridge Peak looked down on us through clouds of blown snow, flecked here and there by the sun, and the air was full of the howling of the storm, a mighty symphony.

We were soon back in our sleeping-bags, hatching out future plans. In the autumn, Hermann wanted me to come with him on a double-traverse of Mont Blanc, by all its great ridges. Then, the following year, perhaps, we would have a go at Rakaposhi . . .

Towards evening the barometer began to rise again and we cheerfully fell to packing our things for the morrow. Then it suddenly cleared, and through the entrance to the tent we saw Baltoro Kangri, sublime in the light of the evening sun . . . we might climb it after Chogolisa . . .

The Last Day

June 27th dawned clear, fine and calm, a veritable gift of the Gods. We were happy beyond words. Our rest-day had done us good, and we felt brimming over with fitness, and a burning zeal to bag the summit.

We were off at about a quarter to five. It was still very cold, but we knew it couldn't be for very long. The sky grew lighter and lighter above Baltoro Kangri. To the south lay a sea of summits, peaks about 20,000 to 23,000 feet high, and hardly even explored. To the north the sun was already touching K2. Between us and it, Broad Peak displayed only its main summit, masking the other two.

Almost as soon as we had got our legs moving, the warmth of the sun reached us. We tramped happily up over the glittering snow. Free of our loads, we made unbelievably easy progress. The going was excellent on the very crest of the ridge, but the snow was deep and trying on either side; besides which, the wind had formed dangerous wind-slabs on the slope. One of them broke away quite close to us and went thundering down in a fair-sized avalanche to the level plateau of the Kaberi Saddle below. It made quite an impression on us and we stuck carefully to the crest of the ridge, which was so far uncorniced. But how would things go up there on Ridge Peak, where we could see cornices several yards wide projecting unpleasantly in a continuous hem? No doubt the storm of the previous day had notably increased their size.

At 23,000 feet we left the ridge, by now corniced, and traversed a little way across a smooth ice-slope to reach a projection farther up. There were actually a few rocks here, quite a curiosity on this mountain. And what about the route above? Ye Gods! There was the summit, just over there! It couldn't be any great distance and it certainly didn't look difficult. We ought to be up on it by midday, we thought.

Indeed, the next bit was easy; the slope flattened out appreciably and all we had to do was to keep along it to the deep notch beyond Ridge Peak. We made light of turning the huge cornices which towered over us to the right. Chogolisa's immense roof drew rapidly nearer, but after a quarter of an hour we had to admit it wasn't going to be easy. The slope grew steeper and the sector of ridge rising behind it had a distinctly airy look. Then suddenly we could see the whole route, and there was nothing about it to be lightly dismissed. The ridge down to the notch was as sharp as a knife-blade, its left-hand side a giddily steep precipice of rock and ice, to its right great cornices hanging far out over the North Face. We should have to be very careful there. The rock precipices below us kept on forcing us farther up towards the jagged white crest. We belayed carefully with the rope, watching for avalanches. A small wind-slab did in fact break away and went sliding away into the abyss. The snow conditions were really a curse. Just as we got to the rocks, Hermann went through to his waist, and hardly had he scrambled out when he was sitting in another hole. Damn it, the slope was a positive honey-comb! Hermann balanced his way forward as if walking on egg-shells – lucky man, he didn't weigh much. He reached ice-plastered rocks and moved from foot-hold to foot-hold with incredible delicacy of balance, hardly touching the holds as he moved. A moment later he disappeared over a rib. 'Up you come!' I could hear him calling.

Rope's length by rope's length, we worked our way along the ridge, sometimes on the slope, sometimes right up at the edge of the cornices. Steadily, the wind passed over the crest; glittering snow rose towards the deep blue dome of the sky. Down in the south there were huge clouds now. But they did not move.

We had made good time in spite of the unexpected difficulties. It was only 9 o'clock when we reached the saddle at 23,000 feet. And there, only 2,000 feet above us, was the sharp tip of the turret on the long crest of the summit-ridge. A steep, but for the most part broad, ridge of snow led up to it.

We sat down in a sheltered hollow, in glorious warm sunshine, and took off the rope. We were ravenous; what about a drop of tea and those delicacies we had saved up for our trip to the top? 'This is the best day for me since I came out with the expedition,' mused Hermann. How well I understood him. Climbing a seven-thousander in three days . . . not in three weeks!' This was just his pigeon – very different from what he went through on Broad Peak. I shared his obvious delight.

We didn't move on for a whole long hour. When we did, we took alternate leads in deep snow. We were unroped now. It was enough to carry the rope with us in the rucksack, Hermann said, so I did not think much about it. A steep pitch with a short ice-cliff called for work with the axe; after that it was easy again. Occasional cracks in the slope spelled avalanche-danger. They pushed us out farther on to the brink of the precipice than we had intended.

Ridge Peak was gradually sinking below and behind us. To the south, the great mountainous banks of cloud were moving very slowly nearer. The sky was calm and of a deep, deep blue. The banner of snow blowing from Ridge Peak seemed to have grown a little. To the north lay a tremendous prospect: all the giants of the Baltoro lined up in a row, a whole chain of peaks 26,000 feet high or only just less. We let our gaze range in wonderment from K2 to Hidden Peak. We took photographs and then moved on again.

How quickly the clouds were coming towards us now! We hoped they wouldn't interfere with our view from the top. We quickened our pace. The last steep pitch began a little way up there, and close above it we could see the tower that was the summit – 1,500 feet at the most – *that* couldn't take so very long.

Presently a little cloud came climbing up the slope below us. It grew larger, enveloping us, enveloping the peak. Without any warning, all hell broke loose. Grey veils of mist scurried across the ridge. Unnatural darkness swamped us. We fought our way forward through clouds of blown snow, bending double to meet the fury of the gale. On the crest of the ridge it flung itself upon us in full blast, snatching at our clothes, trying to claw us from our footing. It was terribly cold and the needles of ice blowing down into our faces hurt savagely. We could only see the next yard or two ahead. We kept on changing the lead, struggling grimly upwards.

It didn't seem possible. I thought of the blue sky such a short time back. It had all been so quick. I had an uncanny feeling – hadn't exactly the same thing happened to the Duke of the Abruzzi, quite close to the summit? Were we going to be robbed, too? Away with such stupid thoughts; it was only a few hundred feet, and we had *got* to do it.

It grew lighter for a moment, as the wind parted the driving clouds. We stood rooted, looking up to where the summit must be. There it was, near enough to touch, looming darkly above us. An instant later the wrack had swallowed it up again.

The storm continued its horrific din. Laboriously we moved up, with a steep, bottomless precipice below us, keeping close to the ridge crest. Everything was white now and we could hardly see.

We were at about 24,000 feet. Only another thousand to the summit-tower. Suddenly Hermann spoke: 'We've got to turn back at once, or the wind will cover our tracks up, and then we shall stray out on to the cornices!' He was quite right. We hadn't given a thought to it; and now visibility was almost nil.

We should have to hurry. We turned then and there. Hermann had been leading, so I was in front now. He followed at a safe distance of ten to fifteen yards, which was all that visibility would permit.

Bent double, I felt my way downwards. It was incredible – only 150 feet down, there was no trace to be seen of our upward trail, except the deep holes made by our axes. Very soon there wouldn't be very many of *them*. And still the tempest kept up its infernal din.

I reckoned we must be at about 23,600 feet, and that we must be near the steep avalanche slope which had pushed us so close to the cornices. If only one could see a bit more! I turned and saw Hermann coming after me, keeping the distance unaltered, following in my actual steps. As I moved down, I kept on looking across to the left, trying to see through the mist. All I could see was that it was getting a bit darker overhead and a bit lighter below. That must be the edge of the cornices. It seemed a safe distance away, but in mist distances can be deceptive. Perhaps it would be better to keep a bit to the right, but then I should have to look out for the precipice. It ought to be here by now. Ah, there's another axe-hole . . .

I looked anxiously to the left and then down to the surface at my feet. I was at a loss; it was almost impossible to see anything at all. *Crack!* Something shot through me like a shock. Everything shook, and for a second the surface of the snow seemed to shrink. Blindly, I jumped side-ways to the right – an instantaneous reflex action – two, three great strides, and followed the steep slope downwards a little way, shattered by what I had seen at my feet – the rim of the cornice, with little jagged bits breaking away from it. My luck had been in, all right! I had been clean out on the cornice. What would Hermann have to say about that, I wondered? I stopped and turned, but the curve of the slope prevented my seeing over the crest as I looked up. The light was improving a little. Hermann must bob up any moment up there. I still couldn't fathom that extraordinary shaking sensation; had the snow really settled under my weight?

Still no Hermann. 'Hermann!' I shouted. 'For God's sake, what's up? Hermann!' I rushed, gasping up the slope. There it was, the crest . . . and beyond it, smooth snow . . . and it was empty . . . Hermann . . . You! . . .

Done for . . .

I dragged myself up a little farther. I could see his last footmarks in the snow, then the jagged edge of the broken cornice, yawning. Then the black depths.

The broken cornice – that had been the quaking beneath my feet, then.

I couldn't get a sight of the North Face from anywhere near. I should have to get down to Ridge Peak for that. As I went down, the storm gradually abated, and the mists lifted from time to time. I was utterly stunned. How could that have happened just behind me? I had the greatest difficulty in getting up the short rise to Ridge Peak, but even before I got there it had cleared up. I hurried out to the farthest edge of the cliffs.

The storm was hunting the clouds high into the heavens. Above the veils of mist and through them a ridge loomed up – a tower – a great roof with tremendous banners of blown snow streaming from it. Chogolisa, the horrible. I could see the spot where we had turned at about 24,000 feet. Our trail down the broad snow-field below was crystal clear. Then that fearsome drop to the north – into the clouds. And there, even closer to our tracks as they ran straight downwards, the encroaching precipice. And then I could see it all with stark and terrible clarity. Just at that point, Hermann had left my tracks at a slight bend, where I was hugging the rim of the precipice, and gone straight on ahead, only three or four yards – straight out on to the tottering rim of the cornice – straight out into nothingness. Of the foot of the wall I could see nothing. Stupidly, I stared upwards again.

If we had been roped . . .

I looked down along the face, shuddering . . .

No, I should never have been able to hold him there; at the moment of his fall I myself was too far out on the overhanging snow.*

At last I could see clearly down below, where the broad snow-masses of an avalanche fanned out. The crashing cornice had set it off and it had swept the face clean. Hermann was nowhere to be seen. He must have fallen at least 1,000, maybe 2,000 feet and was lying there buried under the piled-up snow. Could he have survived that? There was no answer to my shouts and I had no way of getting down there. I should have to fetch the others and we should have to come from below. That was the only faint possibility. I strained my eyes, searching every cranny, searching for a rucksack, a ski-stick, a dark blob. But there was nothing to be seen – absolutely nothing. Only our tracks – up there . . .

Clouds blotted the mountain out again. I was alone.

Mists and a high wind were sweeping the corniced ridge as I tried to find the way down. At times I could see nothing at all and could only tell from rifts in the snow that I had strayed too far down the slope. After what seemed an age, I found our tent. It was a horror of emptiness. I took the absolute essentials for the descent and went on down. At the Kaberi Saddle there was knee-deep fresh snow, through which only a tiny corner of the marker-pennants showed. I probed with my feet under that smooth expanse of white to find out from which side our ascent-route had come, then went straight on into the whiteness . . . to the next pennant. I wandered vaguely down endless hollows, over crevasses, through fog, then into the darkness of night. For long, indescribable hours of horror – during which I at times had a feeling that Hermann was still with me – I managed, by some miracle, to find my way, on-wards, downwards. Then, just before the great ice-falls, my pocket-lamp failed; so I had to bivouac at 18,000 feet. In the first pale light of dawn I made my way down the ice-falls. On and on . . . endlessly on . . . till, 27 hours after Hermann's fall, I tottered into base camp.

The search which followed found absolutely nothing.

Once again, the monstrous rubble-covered river of ice lay freed of all human presence. The sun burned down on it with scorching intensity. The snow was rapidly vanishing, melting into the waters of gurgling glacier-streams. Chogolisa's white roof-tree seemed to lift into the very

* Though, perhaps, the pull of the rope would have kept him in my tracks, and he might never have strayed from the right line of descent. – K.D.

A similar thought was expressed by Othmar Gurtner, commenting on the author's account in *The Mountain World*, 1958–9. – Translator's note.

sky itself. The great peaks stood silently all around. Were they, too, mourning? Or was this only the great healing silence which eternally enfolds all living and dying?

The engines droned as we flew down the Indus Valley, with mountains close on either hand, sharp spires past which we floated. Steep ridges thrusting up; an occasional glimpse back to the giant Baltoro peaks . . . K2, Broad Peak . . . already distant, as the minutes sundered us from the months. We should soon be seeing Nanga Parbat.

My thoughts went back to our inward flight, when the weather had been bad. I could see Hermann's face, as his eyes bored into the grey clouds for a sight of *his* mountain. At last he had spoken. 'We'll only fly back on a fine day,' he said.

Today was a fine day.

The savage peaks ahead parted, and only then did we realize that they were only low wing-pieces to that great stage-setting. High above them there was a shimmer of white; snow banners rose to the heavens. There it stood, the mountain – immutable, immense, imperishable – Nanga Parbat.

We could see its dazzling glaciers, and the summit crowning them. Above it the sky stretched blue-black and deep – as if yet another sky were climbing, incessantly, over and up it – up to an infinity of heights and depths.

Hermann Buhl.

Silver banners, ever-growing up into that dark vault.

PART III

A child was playing snowballs.

It was dirty, grey snow, the last relics of winter on the flower-strewn meadows of a slope, high in the Bernese Oberland. The child ran from one patch of snow to the next, made snowballs and threw them into the flowers, where they broke into glittering dust.

We went on, up over the meadows. Tona, Hilde and I had come up from Grindelwald by chair-lift. It was a gloriously fine day.

Tona is my fair-haired wife. I met her in Milan on a lecture tour; she was studying geology then. We went up into the mountains, we fell in love, we married – three years after my Broad Peak adventure. And now we were taking Hildegard, our equally blonde daughter, on an excursion.

Over there, across the valley, the Eiger stood sombre, only the long sweep of the Mittelegi Ridge and the snow on the very summit brightly lit by the sun's rays, dazzling white, making the North Face seem darker still by contrast.

I would not try it again; once was enough. Yet I understood well enough why I had done it, as I looked up at the Mittelegi, glittering white, and the dark North Face winging upwards.

'Papa – why did you climb the Eiger?' Hilde asked me. Tona was smiling; the green slopes lay warm under the sun. What should I say?

'I can't explain it exactly,' I replied. 'But the Eiger is big and high.'

'M'm . . .' She did not seem very convinced, and nor was I. Then she laughed and started all over again to run from one patch of snow to another, making snowballs, throwing them into the green grass. Ah, thought I, she can't be racking her brains about it any longer . . .

Then, suddenly, she came back, stopped, and looked at me with a little smile. 'Do you know,' she asked, 'why I should like to climb the Eiger?'

'No,' I said, deeply curious now to know. 'Tell me, then.'

She laid that fair head of hers a little on one side, crushed the last remnants of a snowball in her palms, and looking up at the summit with her bright eyes, spoke deliberately, pausing several times, as if carefully weighing the meaning of her words.

'I . . . the Eiger . . . I should go up . . . to make snowballs . . . you see . . . the snow is much whiter up there.'

That is just how she said it.

The North Face of the Eiger

Why do we do these things? Because we enjoy them? Standing at the foot of the Eiger's North Face, I very much doubted it.

A huge, dark triangle rises sheer above the meadows of Alpiglen. There is no life in it, only cold rock. A monstrous slab composed of stone; of grey, riven ice-fields, of crumbling bastions . . . a labyrinth of glassy runnels and ice-encrusted niches between polished steps of rock, rising vertical – like storeys of a house set one on top of the other – right up into the clouds.

That is the Eiger – a world of shadow, ice and silence: a silence broken occasionally by the rattle of falling stones, audible right down to the meadows at its foot.

Rébuffat once described it as 'a stone standing in a flower-garden'. It has never been better described. The base of the 'stone' is two and a half miles long, about half of which is occupied by the North Face. As to its height – if you could lodge the three Zinnen like a child's bricks, one on top of the other, the Western on the Grosse, and the Kleine on top of that – they would still fail to reach the Eiger's summit by hundreds of feet. So it is not surprising that, when you look up it from its base, the ground seems to give way beneath you – for that face is 6,000 feet high.

Six thousand feet . . . between the meadows at its feet and the clouds on its 13,000-foot summit rises a surface which, on the flat, could accommodate a city. Yet, a city is an expression of man's life and activity; the Eiger was not made for human-beings. Because it stands entirely on its own and wide-open to the west, every break in the weather smites it first and with insensate fury. Its inward-curving cavity is like a dark, empty shell tilted against the sky. The clouds which get trapped in it cannot get out again; they cling to the face, circling endlessly between the tremendous ribs enclosing that hollow space, until they eventually dissipate or are sucked up over the summit by the north-westerly gale. Even when the face is clear and windless again, everyone who stands at its foot and looks up into the curved recess feels that something defying

all description lies locked in that hushed amphitheatre. Does that con-
cave face embrace the dimension of death itself; of the negation of
everything?

The Eiger's face was not made for human beings; its artillery of falling
stones strikes blindly. That wall transcends all concepts of battle and
victory, of life and death. At least it did till men came and imported
them. Men who lived and thought there under that hail of stones, in the
whirling fury of the tempest, at the very limits of their being. Men who
sought to penetrate that inhuman dimension of the North Face, by
trying to climb it . . .

It is an unnatural, outsize dimension, beyond human ken. It is also a
dimension whose secret no one can resist.

Certainly I, for one, could not.

Wolfi and I were determined to climb the North Face – we two
together, and alone together; neither of us wanted to do it with anyone
else. For if we understood anything it was that this would stretch us to
the utmost.

During the years when succeeding summers had seen us climbing together in the Western and Eastern Alps, we had become a partnership
on the rope in which each of us knew he could depend utterly on the
other, no matter what situation might arise. A rope like that can
tackle anything . . .

We had become friends.

When we arrived to try our luck, there had been twelve successful
attempts. It might have been thirteen, but no one knew for certain –
Notdurft and Mayer were 'presumed dead' in the exit-cracks. Gonda
and Wyss, too, had all but got to the top, when a small snow-slide swept
them to their death from the last few easy feet of the summit-slope. The
historians had disallowed the climb because they had not actually stood
on the summit of the mountain. So the total remained at twelve, during
which thirty-eight people had reached the summit; seventeen had died
in the attempt. For the last five years before we came, one vain attempt
after another had been made to achieve the thirteenth successful climb.
Stefano Longhi's body was still hanging roped to the face. Nobody had
been able to reach him, for he had died in a rather inaccessible place,
way off the normal route, high up on the level of the 'Spider', that
notorious ice-funnel, from which curving gullies, likewise filled with ice,
reach out into the dark face in all directions like the legs of an insect.

Obviously, Wolfi and I could not shut our eyes to all those facts, and
we were just as anxious to go on living as any one else. Nor did we want
to take any risks – so far as it is possible to avoid them on the Eiger's

North Face. We had always climbed with the greatest care, and now we intended to apply an even greater degree of caution to our formidable task. What we did not intend to do, was to abandon our plan – nor, we knew, would the others who were here with the same objective in mind . . .

And who were these others?

One of the great attractions, when one arrives at the foot of the Matterhorn or Mont Blanc, the Civetta's gigantic wall, the Drei Zinnen or the Bregaglia peaks; as one strolls through the streets of Chamonix or Courmayeur – or, in this case, Grindelwald – is to see who is there; for one knows that one may at any moment meet old acquaintances, climbers with whom one has stood on some peak or other, or even friends whom one has not seen for years past.

So we were soon exchanging greetings with Ante Makohta and the slim, fair-haired Nadja from Ljubljana – Nadja Fajdiga, one of the best women-climbers anywhere, not only in Jugoslavia. They too were waiting for their great chance – settled weather-conditions. Their much-patched, sun-bleached tent was meanwhile pitched on an alp high up near Alpiglen. The only things that could disturb a climber's idyllic peace up there at the foot of the Eiger were cows, and inquisitive people, who wanted to know what the rope was for. And so, as every summer, there were quite a few tents to be seen about the place.

One of them belonged to Hias Noichl, that indestructible guide and proprietor of a ski-school at St Johann-in-Tirol. He and those two cheerful cosmopolitans, Herbert Raditschnig and Lothar Brandler had also set their sights on the Eiger. At the moment, Herbert and Lothar were busy serving savoury rarebits, good solid *Berner Röschti* or a Swiss fondue to the guests of the Hotel Gletschergarten in Grindelwald. To see them in their white jackets and black bow-ties hurrying hither and thither, light-footed – with a smiling 'of course' . . . 'thank-you' . . . 'immediately' . . . 'ready now!' on their lips, you would have thought they had never done anything else in their lives. Today Lothar is a film-producer and Herbert travels the world year in, year out, as a camera-man.

They too were waiting to tackle the Eiger. Their rucksacks were ready, packed; they could exchange their white jackets for anoraks any day, but the weather gave them no encouragement. It had not only to be fine; it had to be settled. For they too wanted to take as few risks as possible – the Eiger was dangerous enough under a blue sky; and even if you wore a helmet, you couldn't crawl under it for complete protection. So they were biding their time, and had gone into the hotel-business for a change.

I saw a quiet middle-aged man sitting in a corner, writing. He had a high forehead and craggy features. It was Heini Harrer, who in the summer of 1938, with his friends, Anderl Heckmayr, Wiggerl Vörg and Fritz Kasparek, had been the first to find the way to the summit up the North Face, after a bitter struggle lasting three days – the last part in appalling weather, but then the Eiger has spared nobody so far in that respect. Now he was working on his history of the North Face, which turned out to be a splendid book and a best-seller, not only in mountaineering circles; for today Frau Schulze in Hamburg and Signor Rossi in Milan have read all about the North Face.* It is not without good cause that so many telescopes are to be seen everywhere around Grindelwald, trained on the Eiger, and surrounded by the gay tribe of holiday-makers.

Does that bother the climbers on the face, as he crouches against the rock, his nose pressed against cold ice, with the stones hailing down on him? Not in the least: he has plenty of other things to worry about.

Our base camp was in the cellar of a carpenter's shop at Grund, just below Grindelwald.

It was an ideal lodging; we were wonderfully comfortable among empty packing-cases and racks, which enabled us to sort and separate to our heart's content the considerable baggage our small expedition had brought along. But first we did something even better; we carried an old armchair, a packing-case and a table out into the garden. There, surrounded by flowers and a variety of vegetables, we could sit in the sun, with the Eiger high overhead. Then we bought a few postcards with harmless views of the neighbourhood – huts up on the alps, the gentlemen who blow the alpine horn, a stream with clouds above it and – yes, we even found one in the end! – Grindelwald minus the Eiger. These we dispatched to uncles and aunts, and to all our near and dear ones who, we knew, might worry if they heard that anyone was on the North Face again. 'We are having a lovely time,' we wrote. 'We have done a couple of amusing climbs and are now resting here. After that we want to do the traverse of a splendid ridge. Don't worry about us.' It was all perfectly true, even the bit about the Schreckhorn-Lauteraarhorn traverse. This was to be our final training-climb before we commited ourselves to the face; a fact we naturally didn't mention.

With us at the time were our friends, Franz Lindner and 'Charlie' Schönthaler. Franz, that calm, imperturbable character, we shall meet again in this book, on the Peuteret Ridge of Mont Blanc. Charlie, a carefree enthusiast in every aspect of life, who came from the Tyrol, has

---

* So has John Smith in Birmingham. In 1959, the translator of this book had the great pleasure of converting Harrer's *Die Weisse Spinne* into *The White Spider*, widely read by the general public here too. – H.M.

just returned with me from the great faces of the Bernina Group. After his very first experience of digging crampons into the sheer ice of the Klucker route on the North-east Face of Piz Roseg, he had struck brilliant form, as we did the North Face of Piz Palü, the North-east Face of Piz Bernina, the ice-nose on Piz Scerscen and, to crown everything, the first-ascent of the *direttissima* on the North-east Face of Piz Roseg's main summit. He was fully qualified for the Eiger, but he knew I wanted to go with Wolfi and fully understood. During the following days he helped me, in the most unselfish manner, to transport all our equipment up to our 'high camp' at the foot of the face, while Wolfi was doing one more climb with Franz. Today Charlie is a ski-instructor, alternating between Australia, Squaw Valley and Kitzbühel and, if you are lucky, you may even meet him in Munich, which is supposed to be his home-town.

There was not much more to be done, now. The rocks of the Wetterhorn glowed reddish-brown in the sunset, but a huge fish-shaped cloud was drifting through the pale sky. Still anything but 'Eiger-weather . . .'

All the same, I wanted to go up with Charlie next day to the foot of the face.

The Bernese Oberland, with its streaming glaciers and proud four-thousanders – Finsteraarhorn, Mönch and Jungfrau – lay under a clear blue sky. The weather looked really good at last.

The long line of the huge Mittelegi Ridge was bathed in sunshine; from the massive rock buttresses at its start in the valley to the shining white of the Eiger's summit, where it ends. A few little tufts of cotton-wool were playing tag in the dark hollow of the North Face. The little red cars of the Jungfrau railway climbed the steep rack and pinion track between the meadows . . .

'Alpiglen!'

Out with my pack . . . and then another sack, and the cardboard-box, and the long sailor's sack, and the carrier-frame . . . the conductor was getting impatient. How could anyone be carting so much stuff with him in a summer-holiday resort?

Luckily, the station-master seemed to understand perfectly; for we certainly couldn't take everything up with us at one go. While the bustle of the trippers faded away and the little train climbed on its way, he stood there, taking stock of our pile of goods. Then he looked at us and muttered: 'The Eiger, of course!' and shook his head. 'If you like, you can park some of it here,' he said. 'I have often done it before.' He straightened his cap and pointed to a door: 'In the corner, on the right there,' he advised. We were only too pleased at the offer; we had been on the point of asking for it. Charlie carried everything we could not manage to the place indicated, while I was tying one sack to the wire-frame.

The stationmaster was still standing there, watching us. He was a slow, comfortable, pleasant Bernese type. 'Many thanks,' we said, when we had finished: 'We'll be back for the rest today.'

'Today or tomorrow, whenever you like,' he nodded. Then he suddenly knitted his brows and looked hard at me. Just as I was beginning to wonder what was coming, he said, very quietly: 'Do you have to do that thing?'

I searched around for words. 'Yes,' I said, ' . . . you see . . .'

'Nowt happened to us as yet!' said Charlie with a cheerful grin. 'Come on,' he said, tapping me on the shoulder.

I was still thinking of the man as we slowly climbed far up the green, flowery slopes; and once, when I turned to look back, I felt sure he was still standing down there, looking up at us.

The sacks weighed a ton, and the ascent was a long one. But what a morning it was: sunny and green, everywhere. This Alpiglen was a lovely corner of the world! In front of us rose a broad tongue of forest; above it the North Face hung like a blue shadow. Not till just under the summit did the sun gild a snowfield, the white veins of ice in dark rock – the very last bit of the climb. There didn't seem to be any distance between it and the sky above.

Lothar, Hias and Herbert must have pitched their tent somewhere in this wood, but we couldn't see it. We meant to site ours much higher up, indeed as high as possible; for it was still a long way from here to the start of the climb, at least an hour by night. We were resting again and, with all this gear to cart, we should have found it much more comfortable to stop here. Then we remembered our friends, whom the vicar of Grindelwald came up to visit one day, with the idea of trying to talk them out of the Eiger. So on we went, up the hill.

We found a tiny, steep-sided patch of grass just below the first slabby steps of the face. This was at 6,600 feet, and no one could get a tent farther up. When we looked up, with our heads tilted right back, we could see, way up there, the big icicles hanging down the greyish-brown wall below the 'Spider'. The summit itself was out of sight, high above.

We used moss and slates to build a level platform into the slope and planted our fabric-house on it. We were protected from any odd stones falling from above by a projecting rock. From here it was no distance to the start of the climb; we could get there without expending any effort.

A few days later, after Wolfi had rejoined me in our 'Alpine Week-end Cottage', as we called it, we enjoyed a really priceless experience. We had

just been checking our supply of pitons, when he suddenly nudged me
and said: 'Look! There's someone coming up!'

I saw a dark figure coming slowly up the slopes, still a long way down.
I recognized a uniform. 'A policeman,' I said. We looked around us,
but there was no other tent, nobody else; there could be no doubt he was
coming to see us. All the way up from Alpiglen, an hour away down
there . . .

'Any guesses, Wolfi?'

'Not a thing.'

The uniformed figure continued to climb resolutely, straight for us.

'Anything to do with your motor-bike?' I suggested.

'Certainly not!' replied Wolfi with an ugly look. 'My motor-bike,
indeed!' Wolfi is very touchy about his skill as a rider.

The facings on the uniform were now clearly recognizable. Another
quarter of an hour or so . . .

Wolfi had an idea. 'Do you think they have put the North Face out of
bounds?' he asked.

'Nonsense!' I retorted. 'Anyway, we'll soon know now.'

Then I had a bright idea. 'Do you think we look like someone else?'

'Possibly,' said Wolfi glancing at me and grinning amiably. 'They
may have seen your passport photo, taken on that machine at the railway station.' Tit-for-tat, for the motor-bike, eh? I thought of that photo.
Never again would I try to save money.

'In any case, don't look so agitated,' said Wolfi. 'Sit down and relax.'

We relaxed, in that expectant frame of mind in which everyone waits,
when the eye of the Law falls on them.

Here he was at last, sweating heavily, touching his cap and assuming an
official attitude.

'Your passports, please, gentlemen!'

Oh, so that was it. We handed him our passports.

He ran his fingers through the pages, looked briefly at me, then at
Wolfi, addressing his question to him: 'You're going up there, eh?' he
asked. He pointed up at the shining curtains, which had been moving
slowly up the face all morning.

'H'm,' said Wolfi. What *can* one say when one has planted a tent at
the foot of the wall?

'It depends on the weather,' I interposed.

Our policemen nodded. 'Yes, I know,' he said and pocketed our passports. 'You can fetch them down in Grindelwald,' he explained, 'afterwards – when you have got back safely.' He paused for a moment,
before adding: 'You see, we always do that nowadays – it often helps us
with the question of identification.'

He wished us good-day most amiably, touched his cap again and turned to go, visibly relieved that it would now be all downhill.

'H'm,' said Wolfi, and made his 'funny' face – thrusting out his lower lip, biting it and creasing his face, as if to laugh. But when he does that it usually means he is not at all happy.

A wild gale was raging across the Oberland. Ice-blossoms formed on the ridges, but it was a glorious day, with the sun flashing on the rocks, marvellously beautiful to look at in the magic clothing conjured by the storm.

We were on the ridge leading from the Schreckhorn to the Lauteraarhorn, in the course of our last training-climb before tackling the face. Franz was still with us, but Charlie had gone home. Wolfi and I had decided to start up at the first opportunity, once we were back in Grindelwald.

When we got there, we heard that Hias, Lothar and Herbert had made an attempt while we were away. They were down below again, after an indescribably difficult retreat, without any assistance from anyone almost all the way. The photographs in the papers showed Hias's face drawn with pain; he had one arm in a sling. They had reached the 'Flatiron', when a small stone falling clear from the Spider a thousand feet above struck him on the hand as he gripped a hold.

Poor Hias – what devilish luck! Now he was in hospital at Interlaken, where they were trying to save what remained of his hand. The hardships of that retreat had left their mark on Herbert and Lothar's faces. They had had enough of the Eiger for the time being. Later on, they worked out a plan to climb the face in winter, when there are no falling stones, when the cold freezes everything into immobility. But Hiebeler and three others beat them to it.

We visited Hias in hospital; it was all we could do for him.

At last the weather had turned fine. The snow high up was melting. The North Face looked even darker than usual, a sure sign that the rock-pitches would be dry, free from snow and ice, and that much easier at least. To balance that, the ice-fields in the middle section would be glassy and tough, with no snow-crust; and more stones would come down by day – the bombardment would only cease at night and into the early morning.

I called up Zürich on the telephone and asked the Met Station if one could trust the weather. 'Well, it was a temporary "high" – not too bad.' Could it last a couple of days? 'It might . . .' What were we to do? Yesterday's report from the Tourist Office had sounded much more promising, and the weather certainly looked good. We decided to go up to our 'high camp' and see what happened. Two days ought to see us through our climb.

We packed up. Everything lay strewn on the grass round the tent – pitons, provisions, ropes. We were starting this very night, so as to be climbing tomorrow. Should we take that ring-piton, it was a bit heavy? How much petrol? The small tin. 'But you *must* take your big gauntlets.'

The result? Enormous rucksacks – much too heavy for Grade V severities; but holding everything necessary for a week on the face – one never can tell . . .

No use: it was simply too much. We stood the rucksacks on their heads and started sifting everything all over again.

The slight, blonde Nadja had come up from her tent. 'I see you're busy packing. Starting up tomorrow, then?' she enquired.

'Yes,' said Wolfi, laconically, and went on rolling up the bivouac-bag. It just had to get smaller, somehow.

'O.K.,' said Nadja. 'Then I'll go and cook you a real meal.'

Darkness and silence. Somewhere up there the face frowned on our tent, unseen, but seeming to claw down into it with invisible fingers. We had set the alarm for midnight – for we wanted to be early on our way. Slowly, the minutes ebbed.

We were taking twenty pitons, five of them for ice; an equal number of carabiners; two 130-foot ropes, one of them a light reserve one, in case a retreat was forced on us; a quarter of a pint of petrol, for the small extra-lightweight cooker – enough for five days if it came to the worst; also the rest of our equipment, well tested on any number of face-climbs. Our provisions, weighed to the last ounce, concentrated and worked out more than ever on this occasion, consisted of a small bag of corn-flakes, baked in sugar, nuts and raisins – about two pounds in all. A handful of this special food keeps one satisfied for quite a time – possibly it swells in one's stomach. For the rest – fruit juice, chocolate, glucose and quite a hunk of smoked bacon, filling and satisfying; add a little bread, a luxury if one considers its weight, but a necessity. Then bivouac candles for the night; for if anything was certain, we should have to bivouac. A few other trifles . . .

I had fallen into a deep and dreamless sleep. I woke and looked at the dial. Still an hour to go. Well, I was hardly likely to sleep any more, now.

I got out the sketch of our route and quietly turned on my torch, laying my hand over it with great care, for Wolfi was still asleep. A narrow crack of light glowed red between my fingers . . .

It was a fairly large photograph of the face, on which we had pen-
cilled in the route. I skipped the first 2,600 feet of the plinth, with its
horizontal stratification. It was not difficult, and we wanted to deal with
it before daybreak; Wolfi had been up it during an attempt last summer;
he knew the way. After that massive stratified plinth, there are 3,000
feet of sheer and at times vertical rock-face, with long traverses to be
made, gaining little height and costing much time and labour. In the
central section we would have to cross the three ice-fields, steep as church
roofs, each of them poised above vertical cliffs, and with their ice
pitched at from 55 degrees to 60 degrees. The traverse of the second ice-
field in itself is a matter of twenty rope's-lengths. During all this, the
main danger is from falling stones, from which there is no respite till,
after the third ice-field, one reaches the 'Ramp'; there they fall clear
through thin air, missing it in their flight. After that, we should have to
take great care not to continue too straight up the face, as Mayer and
Notdurft did last year, and Longhi and Corti too, a mistake to be
avoided at all costs. Our job would be to find the 'Traverse of the Gods',
a crumbling ledge leading to the Spider's huge funnel. Once through
that, another place demanding the greatest care; for, above the Spider
there are countless runnels, cracks, twisting gullies, not all of which take
one out to the summit.

Yes, we would be taking that photograph with us and looking after it
as if it were a talisman; for if mists and blizzards robbed us of all visibility, it would be our only guide to escape from the face. On it we could
measure rope's lengths with our fingers, find the route, either up or
down; for there is no way of getting out of that enormous shell to left or
to right. I folded the picture up carefully and put it away.

A quarter of an hour to go. In the red light glowing through my
fingers I held a small medal, its dull gleam bitten into by tiny lettering.
Busle had given it to me when we parted. The Protestant Paternoster in
English: 'For Thine is the Kingdom, the power and the glory, for ever . . .'
Her prayer – she was a Protestant. To me it was not less precious for that;
in this whole world there is only one of it.

Overhead, in the darkness, soared the North Face.

Almost midnight, now. I pushed my head out of the tent entrance to
see what the weather was doing. Stars and more stars; not a cloud in the
sky; dew on the grass. The Eiger in impenetrable darkness.

Crawling in again, I shook Wolfi. 'Just on twelve!' I said.

'O.K. – O.K. I know. Just five more minutes . . .'

Presently: 'Is it fine outside?' he asked.

'Yes, a clear sky and dew on the grass.'

'Well, I suppose that means we go. What does the altimeter say?'

'You've got it in your pocket,' I replied, handing him the torch. The brilliance of its beam made me shut my eyes for a moment. 'Well, what does it say?'

'Very odd,' said Wolfi, tapping its dial. 'Ten feet higher than yesterday, and that should mean bad weather. Yet it's really fine, and cold, outside – couldn't look better. The dial could have slipped round in my pocket, or it might just have gone wrong.' We had had trouble with it once before. 'Anyway, I say we should go . . .'

1 a.m. Up over the patches of grass, towards the start of the climb, traversing, going up and down, to the débris-cone we knew rose above us. Every now and then we caught sight of the first crags, in the light of our torches. Above them stretched an impenetrable curtain of darkness, a black mass, whose upper edge cut into the starry sky – immense and unknown. What had we to offer against that? All I knew was that I would not want to tackle it with anyone but Wolfi.

'Here we are!' He had recognized the place from his attempt the year before, when I was in the Karakorum. We climbed the débris-cone and a crag or two till a patch of snow shone white in the beam of the torch.

'There's a slab off to the right, here,' said Wolfi, locating it presently, as the beam moved over the rock. 'Only Grade III!'

I followed him as he crossed the little *schrund,* where the snow had melted, and disappeared up the rocks above. All right! Only Grade III it might be, but with a rucksack weighing a ton . . . no ballet-dancing here.

On we went, up crumbling rock-pitches, ledges, precipitous sandy rubble. It wasn't difficult, but it was damnably tricky work, for we could only see the next few feet ahead in the light of our torches. By 3 o'clock, we were at the foot of the First Pillar, up on our left; we couldn't see it, but Wolfi knew it was there. No moon, only the light of the stars; the mountain was asleep, utter silence reigned on its face. We continued our strange, ghost-like ascent, hardly exchanging a word. Every now and then the beam of one head-lamp or the other slashed through the darkness. Occasionally a stone went clocketing down into the void, reminding us, surprisingly, that the face did not consist merely of a few feet of rock on which one happened to be climbing at the moment, but that there was already a great deal of it below us.

We climbed unroped, each of us alone with the light of his lamp, the sound of his boots on the rock, the feel of his hands on it. From time to time, a flash of light, or a word – the only communication with the other man.

It was 4 a.m. and still dark. 2,000 feet of the face lay behind us. Wolfi stopped at the foot of a step, barring the way, not very high but vertical. 'I don't remember that one,' he said. 'Never mind, let's get up it, and not waste time searching around. Make a back for me.' I planted myself firmly on the ledge. Oops! – and again: we were up, not exactly elegantly, but what did style matter, if we could save time and strength? What mattered was getting as high up as possible before the sun was on the rocks.

Another step, another back-up, this time superfluous.

'Up to the left,' said Wolfi. 'We're above the "Shattered Pillar" now.' And he pointed across to where a profile was looming vaguely out of the first grey light of dawn, the shadowy, threatening overhangs of the 'Rote Fluh'. The stars were paling now – fewer and fewer, till there were only three big ones.

'We'll be at the "Difficult Crack" in a moment,' said Wolfi, as we traversed to the left up the slabs.

The sky turned blue above a red streak on the horizon; not the tiniest of clouds in it. The rocks around us were beginning to reflect the new day. And what a marvellous one!

Wolfi was beaming: 'Suppose we had believed the altimeter!'

'Yes,' I answered. 'It's just like our Matterhorn day!'

What a day that had been! The sun had met us on the ice-field, dazzling-bright, to shine on us all the rest of the day. And as the points of our crampons bit into the snow, we kept on thinking: 'Here we are on the North Face of the Matterhorn, *our* North Face . . . at last . . . and on just such a day as this . . . on the North Face . . .'

And now we were on the North Face of the Eiger.

'You see if we're not the first to get right up the Face in fine weather,' I shouted across to Wolfi, who was traversing along a ledge in the rock, now brightly lit by the reflected daylight. Above us towered the face, smooth and overhanging. It would not be long before we were in deep shadow again.

We came to the Difficult Crack, one of the Grade V pitches. Ten feet straight up, there was a piton below a projecting roof. Wolfi clipped himself on and straddled out on to the slab to its left – cautiously, slowly not altogether easily, for his rucksack was heavy. This was no place for ballet-dancing, no matter how good the climber. By now Wolfi had got to the overhang thirty feet farther up, not a very big one, but . . .

Wolfi was cursing his rucksack: 'Damnable, the way this lump pulls one outwards!' He was panting, and I kept a close eye on his every movement. There, he's done it, he's up! I have never seen Wolfi 'come off' yet; he doesn't like the idea, so he never takes a risk. Of course I belay him carefully in spite of that, but it is a comfortable feeling to be on the rope with him. That is probably why we have climbed together so often.

As it happens I don't like the idea of 'coming off' either.

Wolfi had moved on up, straddling widely in a groove, his red anorak a bright spot in the morning sunlight. I took a picture of him, with the overhangs of the 'Rote Fluh' overhead. The Rote Fluh – a face in its own right, a face in the Eiger's great face, leaning far out over our heads, unclimbable by normal means, impossible.

What must Hinterstoisser and his friends have felt that day, years ago, when they looked up from this point? . . . Would it be possible to traverse below that smooth, solid wall, across to the first ice-field; could they get there without having to climb that first enormous cliff? Would the Eiger unlock its gate for them?

The Eiger unlocked the gate. They found the traverse, that 'Hinterstoisser Traverse', which is the gate to the North Face. And then it locked it again behind them.

For, when they were forced to retreat, they found the traverse – heavily iced by the break in the weather – impossible to negotiate; a withdrawal over its glassy slabs is only feasible if the traversing-rope is left in position . . . and they had taken it with them . . .

Very soon we should have dealt with the first 2,600 feet of this gigantic face. It was by now 7 a.m. Everything down in the valley was bathed in sunshine, the meadows shone green, the houses in Grindelwald small and cosy. Where we were, it was cold and grim. We were out of the sun now, and there was ice wedged between the rocks in places. The climbing was not hard and we gained height rapidly; but the area of what was climbable was continually shrinking, swallowed up by the might of the Rote Fluh above us and ahead of us and by the rim of the fearsome precipice pushing up on our left. Finally, it narrowed to a wedge of a snow-crest and then – petered out.

We were out on the smooth sweep of the face, surrounded everywhere by almost vertical slabs. The first few feet were covered by a veneer of ice, above which we could see a piton and an old hemp-rope, curving out in a wide loop, then disappearing from view. 'One of its strands is broken,' growled Wolfi.

That rope had been hanging there for a week, ever since the retreat of the Hias, Lothar, Herbert trio. Poor Hias . . . all because of these blasted stones! All hell must break loose here when the sun is shining on the upper part of the face; the slabs and the rounded limestone cliffs are in places scored with a network of white scars where the stones have struck. At the moment all was quiet. 'A somewhat hostile district,' growled Wolfi, and moved off with great care out on to the slabs.

The Hinterstoisser Traverse is 130 feet long. Wolfi had disappeared from view. Out ran the rope in little jerks, quicker than I had expected, but then the rock was dry and in excellent condition. It was a hot summer and so the Eiger was 'dark' for us, and I have already explained the advantages and drawbacks of that – easier climbing on the difficult rock sectors because they are free from snow and ice, but heavier falls of stone, and tough polished ice, hard as glass, on the ice-fields above.

I could just catch Wolfi's 'come on!' from the far end of the traverse. It is a most impressive place. Below me was an appalling drop of 2,600 feet to the meadows, above me 3,000 feet more of the face. Between the two there was a rope, a piton and a small stance, on which I rejoined Wolfi.

He looked at me and said: 'I'll go on, as far as the "Swallows' Nest".' It was almost a question, but he had already hung a sling into the next piton. 'All right,' I said. 'I'll take over from there.' He moved up on the piton, while I belayed him.

'Don't forget to retrieve the sling – it's ours. I don't want to waste any time here,' he called down, almost as if apologizing for his technical inelegance; the pitch really didn't call for a sling, he could have climbed it 'free'. But now time was of the essence . . .

The Swallows' Nest. There we sat, with our legs dangling over nothingness. I tried to spot our tent, without success. Anyway, we had to be moving on. So, on with crampons, for the ice-field. It was my turn to lead now, even if it would have been pleasant to sit in this nice, comfortable niche a little longer . . .

'It's as exposed as any face in the Dolomites,' Wolfi remarked, adding: 'Rebitsch was the first to get down safely from here.'

I tightened my crampon-straps a little, looking down into those blue depths at the same time. It was from somewhere round here, it occurred to me, that Toni Kurz had made his last despairing effort to reach the rescue party below. From here he had let himself down, with the last failing remnants of his strength, on the rope, still ready – the only survivor of a party of four – to fight for his life; let himself down (and I leaning out as far as I dared, could see no end to it, for down there the face overhung) to within six feet of his rescuers, where the knotted rope jammed in the carabiner . . .

Six feet from succour and life . . . and there it all ended . . . there Toni Kurz fell backwards on the rope and died.

Wolfi was addressing me: 'I thought you said you wanted to take over the lead?'

'So I do,' I said. 'I'm off – but watch me carefully up the first few feet.'

Those first few feet were steep slabs of limestone scoured absolutely smooth; the ice-field must have been much bigger at one time and this was its old, polished floor. I remembered the description: 'Millimetre precision work for a pedant'; it really was abominably smooth hereabouts. I breathed a sigh of relief when at last I was able to dig my points into grey ice. It was tough and in places smooth as a mirror, but they managed to grip. Bless the blacksmith down in Grindelwald who let us use his emery-wheel!

If only we had not got to climb rock to get up to the second ice-field, and so blunt the new, keen edges on our spikes! Yet it didn't look very promising without crampons; a barrier of solid rock, down part of which comes pouring a kind of frozen waterfall – a glistening curtain of black, glassy bubbles – the 'Ice-hose'.

We decided it was better to try the dry end of the barrier, without crampons. Wolfi started up it, climbed the first few feet, disappeared over an edge, said something about slabs, then complete silence. It must have got hellishly difficult up there. The rope kept on coming down, going up again, down again, up again. Somewhere up on that roof Wolfi was obviously hard at it, but the waiting seemed endless. There was, of course, the view to look at, nice green meadows down below; but what in God's name was going on up above? Wolfi had stopped moving altogether; only a few fragments of ice came tinkling down. The sun was gradually invading the rocks high up near the West Ridge, but as yet not a stone had fallen, though it was half past eight. What on earth could be the matter with Wolfi?

As I went up, five minutes later, I found out. It was a thing like a steep roof, covered in places by a thin skin of polished ice. I looked diagonally downwards . . . not a pleasant place to go sliding down . . . At last I got up to Wolfi, on a bad stance, with a fairly useless belay – but the only one available. 'I shall be glad when we're away from here,' he confided.

We could see the second ice-field above us, a gleam of greyish-green. All I could think of at the moment was that, up there, one could bang pitons in anywhere one liked. But we had to get there first . . .

A tongue of ice stretched down towards us, but at least thirty feet overhead. Till then there was only a glittering, glassy layer of black water-ice, less than an inch thick, on the solid rock. Not a hope of fixing a piton or cutting a step in that. As I put my crampons on again I couldn't help thinking how stupid we had been to get ourselves into this hole: if we had only kept on, up to the right! Well this is where we were, so thinking wouldn't do any good . . .

'I'm off,' I said.

'Yes – and you know . . .' Wolfi indicated the rope, lying loose in his hand, by a movement of his head.

Yes, I knew well enough what kind of a belay it was.

I placed my crampon against the glassy surface. Could I get a purchase? No, not here. What about there? Yes, there. Now for the next step: I had managed to clear a grip for my left hand. I moved up. The layer of ice was a little thicker, and I moved a step higher on it. I found another place where my spikes gave me a purchase. The seconds went ticking away, each of them vital, none of them bring any respite. Each of them might have been an hour, or more. Here was the slab, the little hollow in the ice, and here was my foot. The only thought in one's mind, how to put it down properly. Good: that one had got a firm hold!

After an eternity there was proper thick ice, good enough to cut a hand-hold, but lying hollow over the rock, giving out a dull sound; not thick enough for a piton, it would simply shatter. Up again, another hand-hold – getting better now.

And then, at last, decent ice. In went a piton. I gave a sigh of relief, so did Wolfi. The world immediately looked a friendlier place.

'Just a moment's rest,' I said, 'then I'll move on.'

'Yes, you take a rest, by all means.'

I took a rest, looking at the piton, the ring, the snap-link, the rope and the grey ice before me. God, those last minutes had been quite a thing!

I went on resting. There was a niche in the ice up above, followed by a crack at the side of a rock-rib. That must be the best line to take. Off I went again.

I reached the niche, a hole in the ice, through which I hung a sling – an additional belay; then came the crack, which went easily, backing-up between ice and rock. As I emerged, I could see the steep slope of the second ice-field just ahead.

'Only another twenty feet,' I shouted down to Wolfi.

There was a little rock-island just above me, which I should be able to use as a stance. I treated myself to the luxury of cutting a couple of steps, great big comfortable steps . . . the ice splintered, the fragments clinked as they flew, till their sound died away down below; potsherds, tough and glassy, toughened by the cold and the eternal shadow which enveloped us.

Sssssssssssss . . .!

A stone whizzing past, not very far off – the first sign of life on the face. Then all quiet again, here in the shadow; utter silence. High above, rock and snow lay bright in the sunshine, quiet, peaceful, warm-looking. And that was precisely where the menace hung – the menace that could at any moment shatter the cold silence down here, the menace of that beautiful warm glow.

Tick . . . tick . . . ssst. Just a baby stone, hopping harmlessly, dancing down the rocks, whispering past like an insect, small and no danger to anyone. But how long before the cannonade would start, to shatter the peace and quiet down here? It could be minutes, it could be half an hour . . . It was 9 a.m.

I looked up at the warm, even light on those rocks. Then I started cutting steps again, smaller ones, quicker than before. I was up. In went a piton and then I hacked out a stance.

I shouted down to Wolfi: 'You can come now – but look out! The first stones are arriving.'

'So I noticed,' came up from below. 'One has just gone past me.'

Wolfi was coming up – the traverse, the piton, retrieving the sling, pushing a leg into the crack, reaching up with his arm. At that moment there was a 'click' on my helmet, and I enjoyed an instant's satisfaction at the thought that I was wearing it. Then Wolfi joined me.

'We'll have to get up there before it really starts,' he said, pointing to the upper rim of the huge ice-field. He was right; there seemed to be at least a measure of cover under the jutting cliffs up there. We should take much longer by following that long curving rim than if we traversed diagonally, but –

'Look out! Something's coming!' Wolfi, six feet above me, reacted instantly, pressing himself hard into the ice. A host of little dots was coming down in a grotesque dance across the grey surface 300 feet higher up. They grew larger, bounding down towards us in great leaps, a grey army of them. Now! . . . that one's missed me, and that one, but what about this one? . . . sssst, ssst . . . Suddenly everything was quiet again. It was all over.

Wolfi straightened up slowly. 'Benediction over?' he asked. 'Then I'll lead on again. You keep watch and shout if you see anything coming.'

I cast an anxious eye up the face, the surface of the ice, the groove running up to the rocks above. Nothing stirred. The rope ran out quickly, as Wolfi went diagonally up the next 130 feet. He dispensed with step-cutting; we had to get out of the line of fire as quickly as possible. Tack . . . tack . . . tack, his crampons bit into the smooth surface, tilted at 50 degrees or more. It looked uncanny.

The view down the face had completely disappeared; all we could see was the lower edge of the second ice-field projecting over the abyss like a ski-jumping platform, with green ground beyond it, sending up a pale green reflection, mirrored by the surface up here, making the blue shadows look even colder.

We wondered whether we had been spotted yet. Not that it makes the slightest difference. There is no place on earth where one is so utterly alone. I squinted up the runnel to where Wolfi stood, with only the frontal points of his crampons biting into the steep, bone-hard surface. I stooped and took a tighter hold on the rope.

Everything else had lost all meaning. Wolfi was standing up there on four steel spikes. Whether they held or slipped depended on his next movement . . .

We were alone . . . alone with the North Face of the Eiger. At that moment even our friends had ceased to exist for us.

Down at the Kleine Scheidegg, Herbert had his eye to the big tele-scope. 'I've got them,' he shouted. There, in the black circle of the lens, small and forlorn against the huge face, with a few cloud-tatters floating around it, he had seen two tiny dots against the grey belt of the second ice-field.

Fritz von Allmen, the hotel proprietor, one of the greatest Eiger-experts, who had followed our climb for a long time past, joined him. 'Midday – much the worst time for falling stones,' he commented.

'Yes, it's sensible of them to be keeping to the upper rim, in the shelter of the rocks, till they get out on to the Flatiron,' said Herbert, adding ruefully: 'I wish them better luck than we had!' Lothar was with him; they had come up from the valley as soon as they heard some-body was on the face. They did not know, of course, when we intended to start, but they were pretty sure that we were the two dots they had detected on the face . . .

We were now deep inside the great shell, working our way up to the end of the ice-field; in sunshine now, and it was warm. Water was trickling down the rocks, the ice was softer and had acquired a crust.

The hail of stones was nerve-racking, coming irregularly: short gaps, positive barrages, isolated salvoes, then utter silence once more; one never knew what to expect. We made use of every available inch of cover, pillars, pitches of rock, overhangs, crannies. Looking up for a moment at the crumbling bastions high overhead during some interval in the bombardment, we felt little surprise at the unnerving whistle of the falling stones, the sharp crack as they struck on rock, the dull thud when they hit the ice.

At this point the dirty grey surface of the ice-field looked like the face of a man scarred by small-pox. During the fearful minutes of the un-protected moves from one source of cover to another, we were painfully aware of every inch of our bodies. If it had been possible to hide our-selves completely under our helmets we would have felt a great deal better.

Our method of progress was an unusual one – a gigantic hanging-traverse of ice, on a rounded edge formed by the melting away of the ice field's upper rim from the rock above it. For the most part we only supported ourselves against it, for it was by no means all of it solid enough to stand anyone leaning out from it. That traverse across the second ice-field is twenty rope's lengths – more than 800 yards long. You have to grab it a hundred times, move up a hundred times, always with the same extreme care.

I looked up. Bang! Something hit me in the face, blinding me. By sheer instinct I leaned forward against the face. 'It's finished', I thought.

My eyes opened again. There was blood running down my anorak. I put my hand tentatively to my face . . .

Wolfi had me on the taut rope, as I worked my way, bemused, up to a safe stance. Nothing much, he assured me, only a scratch. A small stone had hit me on the bridge of the nose. Just a small stone . . .

My head was buzzing. 'Come on! Off this damned ice-field!' I was still digesting my shock, but Wolfi was already balancing over the irregularities of the icy edge. No time for rest and recuperation sessions here, he said; it was the last thing I wanted, anyway! Wolfi led the next two rope's lengths.

By the time we were traversing out on to the Flatiron, I was quite myself again. At last we were off the second ice-field. For which relief much thanks.

The arête of the Flatiron, 250 feet high, jutting out like a regularly curved nose from the furrowed face, lies directly beneath the Spider and is, consequently, more than usually exposed to the hail of stones. Climb-ing simultaneously, we hurried up its easy rock and sat down, to get our breath back, under a small overhang near the top. Here we were really safe, and we could actually sit. We had now been engaged in fourteen unbroken hours of climbing.

We were ravenous, as we got bacon and bread out of the rucksack. There was even water, dripping down the rock. Now that we were sitting here and the tension was lifted, we could feel the weariness penetrating our bones. We had been on our feet since 1 a.m. and now it was half past four in the afternoon. We were not likely to get much farther today, but there seemed nothing to stop our reaching the summit tomorrow, if only the weather held.

That was the only question in our minds as we watched the little puffs of cloud all around us, climbing up the face, growing in size, disappearing – dissolving into thin air.

Shimmering curtains – as if the spirits of the air were engaged in a grotesque, swirling dance in the void all around us, accompanied by the thousand voices of the North Face, from the high, almost barking whirr of the smaller stones to the less frequent dull growling and roaring of the big lumps. And, somewhere, there was the sound of water pattering down the face.

We were climbing the steep Ramp, which slashes a way up the unbroken cliffs, anything from vertical to overhanging, below the Spider. It was getting late; soon it would be dark. We wanted to get to the good bivouac-site we had heard of, above the most difficult pitch in the Ramp, the famous chimney, which was either filled by a waterfall or by its frozen counterpart. It seemed a doubtful project. Behind us, through the mists, we looked across the tilted roofs of the two ice-fields to a fabulous view; but beyond it lay the veils of dusk. Here, on the steep Ramp, with nothing but sheer cliffs and a snow-gully all around us there wasn't even room to sit down. We should have to push on till we found a place. We got out our headlamps and our torches. By a stroke of luck we found a small hollow in the rock at the end of the first rope's length; there was just room for two people to sit, close together.

We made our preparations for the night very slowly and methodically (this is a long-standing item of bivouac-lore: the longer you take over the preliminaries, the shorter the night) hammered a couple of pitons firmly into the rock, bashed the sharper projections till they were more rounded, melted snow for a hot drink of fruit-juice. Ironically, there was water pattering down, a few feet above us in the darkness; but neither of us felt like climbing another inch. Before pulling the bag over our heads, we took a last look at the lights sparkling down in Grindelwald, more than 8,000 feet below; we agreed that it must be much more comfortable down there, and wondered whether we should be looking down on it from the summit tomorrow. Mists were creeping up from below; the lights wavered, grew dim, disappeared. The night air breathed coldly on us. We sat down and pulled our protective tent-covering over us.

The first light of a new day was filtering through our perlon shell. The night had been quite bearable, in spite of the stones which had refused to surrender their sharpness and the smallness of the sitting-room. Only once did I have to wake Wolfi up, when I heard him say: 'Uncomfort-